The publisher and the author assume no liability for any injuries caused to the reader that may result from the reader's use of content contained in this publication and recommend common sense when contemplating the practices described in the work.

The old-fashioned remedies in this book are historical references used for teaching purposes only. The recipes are not for commercial use or profit. The contents are not meant to diagnose, treat, prescribe, or substitute consultation with a licensed healthcare professional. New herbal recipes should be taken in small amounts to allow the body to adjust.

LLEWELLYN'S

MAGICAL
SAMPLER

The Best Articles from
the Magical Almanac

Llewellyn Worldwide
Woodbury, Minnesota

FIRST EDITION
First Printing, 2015

Book design by Bob Gaul
Cover design by Lisa Novak
Cover illustration and interior art by Sam Guay
Editing by Ed Day

Llewellyn Publications is a registered trademark of Llewellyn Worldwide Ltd.

Library of Congress Cataloging-in-Publication Data
Llewellyn's magical sampler: the best articles from the magical almanac.—First Edition.
    pages cm
  ISBN 978-0-7387-4562-6
1. Magic. 2. Occultism. I. Llewellyn Publications
  BF1587.L54 2015
  133.4'3—dc23
                        2015007856

Llewellyn Publications
A Division of Llewellyn Worldwide Ltd.
2143 Wooddale Drive
Woodbury, MN 55125-2989
www.llewellyn.com

Printed in the United States of America

Contents

AIR

FIRE

WATER

Magical Sampler Thematic Content Guide

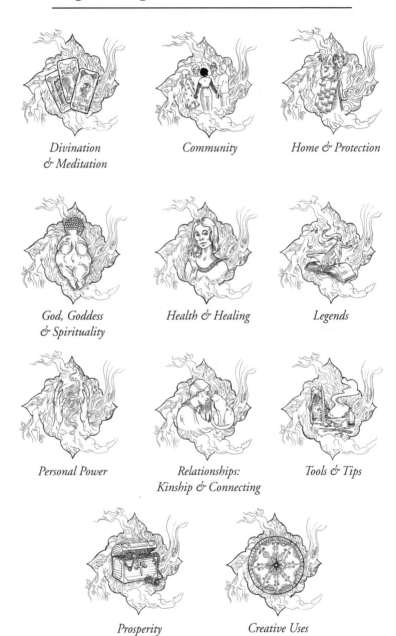

Divination
& Meditation

Community

Home & Protection

God, Goddess
& Spirituality

Health & Healing

Legends

Personal Power

Relationships:
Kinship & Connecting

Tools & Tips

Prosperity
& Abundance

Creative Uses
& Wheel of the Year

Introduction

The Magical Almanac: A Brief History

What started as a showcase for the ideas of well-known magical practitioners has turned into a thriving community of magical people with a wide range of experience and know-how sharing their insights.

The earliest editions of *Llewellyn's Magical Almanac* featured the work of luminaries such as Scott Cunningham, Ray Buckland, Patricia Telesco, Donald Michael Kraig, and Ted Andrews providing words of wisdom to help foster interest in Wiccan and Pagan culture. At the time, many did not know what to make of the small but dedicated community.

As the community grew, so did acceptance. Many people found that they could incorporate elements of Wicca and Paganism into their everyday lives—simple rituals could be done during a coffee break—and no one else had to know! With spirituality being incorporated into basic hobbies and interests like herbs, cooking, nature, and the study of world history, activities once considered arcane and misunderstood, such as yoga and meditation, have become mainstream.

Later editions of the almanac have highlighted writers relatively new to the craft, including those who limit their craft to a specific niche like herb magic but are otherwise in the broom closet, as well as longtime practitioners. Readers have found that having multiple perspectives on a subject has helped shape their craft in ways they hadn't thought possible. Likewise, people who had specialized in a specific type of magic have found ways to cross over and try something new.

This brings us to this tome. *Llewellyn's Magical Sampler* is a look at some of our most interesting articles over the last twenty-five years. A potent potpourri of rituals, spells, and essays on topics ranging from magical stones, dream interpretation, how to use lint as a tool, music in ritual, enhancing your creativity, magical baths, and the legends of Wales.

The Magical Almanac has always strived to be inclusive—the words you read could be those of a neighbor or a noted sage on any given topic. And because new ideas have always been encouraged, the almanac has helped launch the careers of many writers. You may find that while absorbing new takes on old ideas, the synergy may result in a new idea of your own.

However, there are no guarantees. All you can do is relax and enjoy the journey.

EARTH

The Magic of Talismans

......

by Raymond Buckland

A talisman is a man-made object endowed with magical powers, usually either for protection or for bringing luck, in one form or another, to the bearer. The Hermetic Order of the Golden Dawn stated that a talisman is "a magical figure charged with the force which it is intended to represent." Donald Michael Kraig, in his book *Modern Magic*, defines a talisman as "any object, sacred or profane, with or without appropriate symbols, which has been charged or consecrated by appropriate means and made to serve a specific end."

Talismans may be used for any aspect of health, wealth, love, or luck. Similarly, they may be made of virtually any material, though there are traditional materials preferred by serious magicians. These are as listed below, together with the days of the week they are associated with and the properties associated with them:

Talisman	Planet	Day	Property
Gold	Sun	Sunday	Fortune, hope, money
Silver	Moon	Monday	Merchandise, dreams, theft
Iron	Mars	Tuesday	Matrimony, war, enemies, prison
Mercury	Mercury	Wednesday	Debt, fear, loss
Tin	Jupiter	Thursday	Honor, riches, desires, clothing
Copper	Venus	Friday	Love, friendship, strangers
Lead	Saturn	Saturday	Protection, life, building

It can be seen from this that a talisman for love would be best made of copper and made on a Friday in the hour of Venus. Certainly this would give that particular talisman its greatest impact. However, if it is not possible to get copper, the talisman could be made on parchment without subtracting too much of its potency. Similarly, what should be a gold talisman could be made of copper; a lead one could be of tin; or any one of them could be done on parchment. But for greatest potency and best chance of success, the listed metals, days, and hours should be adhered to. Mercury, of course, is a liquid metal and not a good choice for engraving. These days aluminum is frequently substituted.

The shape of the talisman is not generally important; most are done on coin-size discs and worn suspended on chains about the neck. They can, of course, also be made of rings.

What is engraved, or drawn, on the talisman depends entirely on the objective. It should certainly be first personalized by putting the name of the person on one face. A talisman is best made by the person who is going to use it. You can certainly make one for someone else but it will never be as effective as one he or she makes. The reason is the same as for any other form of magic; the person most directly concerned is the one who will put the most power (mana) into the ritual, and thereby into the talisman.

Also on the talisman, place a symbol for that which you desire. If you're working for money, dollar signs will do; if for matrimony, wedding bells; if for health, a picture of someone running or leaping about. There are more traditional symbols and sigils that can be used. These are found in many of the old grimoires or books of magic.

Use of one or other of the so-called secret magical alphabets is encouraged. This way you will be working with figures that are not familiar to you, and therefore will be concentrating more and thereby putting power into what you are working on.

When the talisman has been completed it should be consecrated by dipping it into sacred (salted) water and then holding it in the smoke of incense. This should be done while boldly stating its purpose. The talisman should be made in the appropriate phase of the moon and then worn next to the skin for at least seven days.

SACRED ARCHAEOLOGY

······

BY CHAS S. CLIFTON

Many people know that Stonehenge and other European megalithic monuments appear to have served as astronomical and ritual calculator. But controversy still surrounds the suggestion that
a series of archaeological sites in the American West may represent
an attempt to create similar ritual calendars.

The sites of the Ogham corridor—the nickname of a swath
of land reaching from the Oklahoma panhandle into south-
eastern Colorado—do not involve huge standing stones. But
a group of researchers thinks they have a Pagan European origin, an idea that violates conventional American history and
enrages many archaeologists.

And in a time when Celtic art, music, and spirituality are all
enjoying renewals, perhaps it is only these sites' remoteness that
has protected them from being overrun by seekers of ancient

wisdom. Certainly they pose an intriguing question: did pre-Columbian explorers enter mid-North America as much as two thousand years ago? And did they stay long enough to make astrological observations connected to their religious practices? The answers to such questions are, at best, merely conjectural.

The Ogham sites are regarded suspiciously by most archaeologists. One reason is that American archaeologists are not trained to interpret ancient writing, mainly because there is no other evidence of any existing on this continent. Instead, there archaeologists look for artifacts, and so far none have been found in the area that are not believed to be made by prehistoric Indians or by more recent settler. True, a Roman coin once turned up when a septic tank was being dug in the nearby town of Springfield, Colorado, but skeptics point out that you can buy Roman coins cheaply from any coin dealer, and therefore, it could have been planted at a much later date than ancient times.

The situation is similar to what happened with the idea of a Norse settlement in America. For centuries, scholar had puzzled over the accounts in the sagas or Atlantic travel in the Viking Age, and they were skeptical over the ideals that famed Arctic explorer Fridtjof Nansen laid out in his book *In Northern Mists*. Yet only until indisputable Norse artifacts were found in the 1960s in Newfoundland, proving that a village had existed there, were the North American archaeologists convinced.

At least those voyages had been described in a fairly reliable oral and then written tradition. Nothing similar exists describing voyages of Carthagian or Iberian Celitc explorers two thousand years ago—nothing except a series of rock inscriptions along the Arkansas River in Oklahoma and Texas, inscriptions that most archaeologists prefer to attribute to ancestral American Indians.

In fact, if you suggest to many archaeologists that explorers from ancient Libya (the ancient Carthaginians) or the Iberian peninsula (some of whom spoke a Celtic language before it was replaced by Latin) came to American, you might be called a "racist." Many nineteenth-century scholars speculated that all evidence of civilization in this hemisphere, whether Mayan temples or the towns of the Mound Builders in North America, was derived from Old World models. These theories, that all civilizations derived from one or two places such as the Near East, were called "diffusionism." Now, modern researchers lean toward the independent invention of civilization in different places, and diffusionism is very much out of favor, its proponents often accused of pushing ideas of racial superiority. But this swing of the pendulum produces an attitude of scorn toward any evidence that ancient travelers might have come to North America.

Suppose that they had. Maverick American epigraphers, students of ancient inscriptions, make one powerful argument. At three particular sites in Oklahoma and Colorado, they claim, inscriptions can be deciphered to predict astronomical events such as a shadow falling inside a cave at a particular spot when the sun rises on the spring and fall equinoxes. In addition, some controversial dating methods developed by archaeologists at the University of Arizona produce dates of two to three thousand years before the present.

Another argument against these particular inscriptions being modern hoaxes is that in many cases the new, sharper-looking inscriptions are dated and signed by a person from the late nineteenth and early twentieth centuries. That much I can attest to myself. A few years ago I sat in a small west-facing cave in the Oklahoma panhandle as the sun sat at the Spring Equinox.

As it disappeared, its horizontal light struck rock knobs that cast slow-moving shadows across the back of the shallow cave. Nearby were cut Libyan letters, which the late Barry Fell—an oceanographer and researcher on ancient seafaring at Harvard University—translated to read, "Enact at sunset the rites of Bel, assembling at that hour in worship." Nearby another inscription in Ogham letters has been translated to read, "The sun six months north; sinks south for space of months equal number." Above the inscription is the "indicator," something like a marked-off ruler cut into the rock. On the equinox, a pointed shadow passed the middle of the indicator. The marked-off increments corresponded to the days before or after the equinox, showing where the shadow falls on each of the days.

At Crack Cave, located a little to the north in Colorado, a similar Ogham inscription reads, "Sun strikes [here] day of Bel." Nearby, again in Old Irish: "People of the sun." And at a ranch not too far away, another cave inscription was translated to read, "The ring along with the shoulder by means of sun and hill." However, nothing significant happened there on the solstice or equinoctial sunrises. Since another inscription nearby seemed to include the world "Lugnasa" (also called Lammas in English), the cross-quarter day between the Summer Solstice and the Fall Equinox, member of the ranch family visited the site several days running at sunrise. On August 8, halfway between those two dates, the rising sun shone perfectly through a square overhand before the cave.

If these inscriptions were made by ancient European and North African visitors—imagine for a moment that they might have been—then what kind of people were they? The "people of the sun" inscription (if that's what it really says) suggests a sort of priesthood, something like the Druids of Gaul and Britain.

To be fair, we have to look at some good arguments against the epigraphers' case. Unlike with the Norse sites, no foreign artifacts have been found at any of the Ogham sites. But then no one has looked for them systematically. There might well have been none to find—for aside from bronze tools or weapons, or possibly iron ones, which rust away, their possessions might all have been biodegradable. The case for the Norse presence in Newfoundland was based at first only on a small stone weight used in spinning thread and weaving it into cloth. The local Indians did not use such a tool.

Next, the location is unlikely. This part of the United States is lightly populated now—and according to conventional archaeology, it was even more lightly populated two thousand years ago. There are no large ruined villages such as those found on the other side of the Rockies at Mesa Verde National Park, only a few rock structures that might have been huts. Why would anyone want to come here? It was arid, rough country long ago even as it is now, and it was not on the way to another more populated area. Why come all the way across the Atlantic to observe the sun's movements in a remote area inhabited by a handful of people?

Could the inscriptions have been made by Indians who learned the writing from visitor to these shores? This is a conceivable possibility, but that only replaces one mystery with a larger one.

In any event, some modern Pagans feel heartened by the presence of the inscriptions. The writing, if that is what they are, suggest a more peaceful interaction between visitors and natives.

Conquering armies, after all, usually do not stop to make leisurely astronomical observations. Although the Norse sagas say that their colonists abandoned "Vinland" after a series of escalating conflicts with the Algonquin Indians, perhaps the "People of the Sun" maintained better relations with the people they met. When you consider that in 1999, the annual Columbus Day celebration in Pueblo, Colorado, the nearest city, turned into an angry confrontation between an Italian heritage group and American Indian Movement counter-demonstrators, it is tempting to think that history could have taken another, less violent turn than the history of the European exploration that we all learned in school.

Lately, the study of "rock art," which includes both inscriptions and pictures made on rock, has become a new growth area in archaeology. Scholars are beginning to move into territory that used to be considered too risky—such as the growing tendency to see some designs as depicting shamanic vision. What is more, younger British and European archaeologists are beginning to take an interest in the possibility of ancient inscription in America. Having had different training—and not having the preconceived notion that "it can't be here" that is exhibited by many American archaeologists, they could be positioned to evaluate these inscriptions more thoughtfully.

In the meantime, some of us continued to wonder: did the People of the Sun ever cross the high plains, following the Arkansas and Cimarron Rivers up out of Oklahoma to a country where the Rockies gamed on this horizon? And if so, what were they looking for? Cities? Knowledge? Visions?

ANCESTOR MEDITATION

......

by Jim Garrison

At some point in our lives, we naturally come to reflect upon the people who came before us—those who in one way or another brought about our existence, or who contributed to the whole process that made us who and what we are.

According to tradition, it is at Samhain that the veils that separate the worlds of the living from those of the departed grow most thin and one might be able to communicate with these spirits. But there are other times when one might wish to commune with the ancestors, to seek their wisdom and support. It is for such occasions that I share this meditation with you now.

Before beginning, prepare a comfortable space to meditate, some place quiet and private that you can use for this work without interruptions or intrusion. Clear the area of distracting things and prepare a sacred space according to your personal methods. Light a plain, white candle in the north and turn off the lights. Sit, facing the candle and looking to the north. Make yourself comfortable, take deep breaths, and relax. Observe the candle flame. Let the flickering light dance across your skin and become the focus of your vision. Feel yourself sink back into your body. Listen for your heartbeat and feel your heart. Relax. Listen to the rhythm of your heart, feel the pulse of your whole body without moving. Feel the movement of your blood, the inner tides and currents of your circulatory system. This is the strongest, most intimate connection we each have with our ancestors. They live on in each of us. We can flow back along the years through this human river. We can remember the lives of our ancestors. Their memories are carried forward within each of us, a buried treasure locked away within our hearts, awaiting for us to see them out, to open ourselves to their ancient songs. We are the sum of all who came before us within our various lineages. Follow this red river back as far as you feel a need to do so, or care to go. Relax. Listen. When it is time, return your focus to the candle flame. Breathe deep and bring yourself back to the here and now. Stretch your limbs and turn the lights back on.

This is a good time to record your experiences in a journal or diary. What did you see, feel, or hear? What insights or gifts did you bring back with you from this journey? Do not be worried should you not have immediate results. Such things can take time to develop the proper circumstances for the right frame of mind to settle into place, and for you to connect with these ancestral forces. The spirits of our forebears do not necessarily spout bad poetry or lecture us about improbable things. This is not the way to channel wisdom from lemurian warlords or any of that stuff. Rather, this is a simple method of respecting the ancestors we all have and of communing, if not communicating, with their essence, which we share within our own very bodies. The point of this exercise is not to channel the words of a dead person, but to reconnect with the powerful currents of our own, individual lineage of ancestors. The results of this practice are more felt than heard. It is the goal of such a meditation to establish a deep rapport or connection to the wellspring of our being, something that strengthens and refreshes our innermost self.

The visions we carry in our blood are the deep memories of our peoples, the secret stories of our own tribes. Each of us is eventually an ancestor—it's just a matter of time.

Magic for Money

......

by Donald Michael Kraig

Before doing the following ritual, you should ask yourself "Do I really need this money?" The fact is, in most cases people need something that money can obtain for them and not the money per se. For example, perhaps you need a car. You might do a ritual to obtain a certain amount of money only to discover that the car you wanted has been sold and there is nothing else in your price range. If you had done a ritual to get a car, it might have been given to you, it might have been loaned to you, or it might have been sold to you at a price you could have easily afforded without additional money. Your ritual for money actually limited the way in which you could have obtained your desire.

Also, do you really need the money, or is it just for something extra that you would like to have? The intensity of the ritual and its success is in part determined by the amount of personal energy that you can put into the ritual. A true need will usually create much more desire and psychic power than a mild want.

Preparation

Let us assume that you need the money and that nothing can replace this need in this instance. Further, let's assume that you need $50. What we will do is design a talisman to bring the money to you.

Get a piece of non-recycled paper. Color it in the hue that you think would be appropriate. Green, silver, and gold come to mind. Now put symbols on it that represent the amount you need. Perhaps just a dollar sign will be enough. Perhaps you will need $50 written on your talisman.

When do you need money? Be sure to include a date for receiving the funds.

You will also need a room where you can be alone for a few minutes and a green candle.

Things to Remember

Just as humans are seen as having three aspects—spiritual, mental, and physical—magic also has three aspects: the physical actions, the mind's processes, and the establishment of a link to the spiritual world. Your magic may be successful if you do not include all three, but it is more likely to be successful if they are all involved.

The ritual below is simply a model. You can base other rituals on it, but remember to use all three aspects in your ritual design. For more details on some of the association involved, see my book, *Modern Magick*.

The Ritual

Money is associated with the planet Jupiter, so do this ritual on Thursday, the day of Jupiter, preferably about three hours after sunset. Have the candle, some matches, and the talisman that you have already drawn in the area of your ritual. Remember, the talisman is nothing but a piece of paper with some writing on it until you charge it with a ritual.

Start by walking a clockwise circle around the perimeter of your workspace. As you do, visualize (vividly imagine) your body leaving a protective barrier of intense, blue light. Walk the circle three times, seeing the wall of blue light becoming more intense with each circling. If you cannot actually "see" the wall, simply know (not believe—know!) that it is there and that you would be able to see it if your astral vision were better. If you prefer to do a different banishing/cleansing ritual, such as the lesser banishing ritual of the pentagram, that is fine. This is a guide, not the only way.

Move to the center of your area and face east. Light the candle and use the appropriate name of God, saying, "Oh Yud-Hey-Vahv-Heh Ehl-oh-heem, I fervently request that you watch over this ritual and grant my desire." Believe this deep in your heart.

Hold the talisman in front of you and call on the appropriate archangel to follow God's desire by saying, "Oh Tzadkiel, send your angels to bring me the $50 by God's will." Believe deep in your heart that this will be done.

Place the talisman in front of the candle and hold your hands over it, palms down. Call on the appropriate angels to follow the archangel's will and charge the talisman by saying, "Oh Chasmaleem, obey Tzadkiel and charge this talisman." Believe deep in your heart that they are doing this.

Now add your own energy to it by visualizing energy going out of your hands and into the talismans as you exhale three breaths. Immediately after, say "So mote it be," and on the word "be," clap your hands over the candle flame, snuffing it out physically but allowing it to remain lit spiritually.

Put the talisman in your pocket and walk the circle you made earlier, only this time do it counterclockwise and see the blue wall fading. As you walk, say "Thank you, eternal spirits, for watching over this ritual. Go in peace and in love." The ritual is over.

Keep the talisman on you or as close to you as possible. When you receive the $50, destroy the talisman by burning it.

A Prosperity Charm
for the New Year
......

by Edain McCoy

The changing of the year has always been a time fraught with
magic, and every culture has its superstitions and lore about how
this brief moment in time should be observed in order to ensure
a happy and prosperous new year. One of the most prevalent of
these customs is that one must start the New Year with money
in his or her pocket if they wish to find any there during the
upcoming year.

To make a magical money charm to attract wealth to your
own empty pockets you will need a small square of green or gold
cloth and a matching ribbon, several coins, a few small cinnamon
sticks, and some patchouli oil. Early on New Year's Eve spend
some time fondling the coins, infusing them with your desire for

prosperity. When you have done this for as long as you can, place a drop of patchouli oil on each of them and place them, with the cinnamon sticks, in the center of the cloth. Pull up the ends of the fabric and tie the top shut. Place the charm in your pocket or purse, which will be with you when the year turns.

At midnight, or whenever else you (or your magical tradition) observe the change of time, hold it tight, and remember that it is there for you, releasing its wealth of magic for the coming year.

Household Magic

......

by Diana Rajchel

Don't expect, after a spell or ten, for your environment to stay static. Nope—a conjured force, even one conjured only within the scope of your mind's eye, still has an effect. I won't break down the particle physics for you because I can't distinguish an electron from a proton, but in utterly unscientific speech, I can tell you this: when you do some magic, you stir the stuff that makes the dust. After some magic, over time, the floors, ceilings, and corners get dirty. Magical dirt differs from plain old dust dirt in that the magical dust bunnies will, over time, develop minds of their own rather than simply menacing you from the depth beneath your bed. Over time, as you practice more and more magic, your home environment will eventually slag you.

In several cases of energy overuse and neglect, some people have reported poltergeist-like activity. The phenomenon is simply the result of unintelligent energies finding an occupation in the absence of magical direction. If you raise energy without a purpose, the energy will make its own purpose. Sometimes, depending on how the energy was initially raised, it develops a sentience, which can result in anything from minor temperature variations to a night-hag phenomena (paralysis when just awaking). Since not all energy can be grounded out easily, some residue is unavoidable. Having the residue behave in a way you don't like, however, is easily preventable. Aside from keeping your energy levels high to normal, you have the additional motivation of preventing any accidents of energetic work that might spook you or other household members.

A practiced witch will perform a house blessing as soon as she moves into a new home. This rite is optimally performed before any furniture or belongings cross the threshold, but a cleansing and blessing will still work even with furniture underfoot.

Many witches repeat this once a year after the initial blessing, although I've found that cleansing works better when repeated more frequently. This may be because I prefer to live in urban, high-traffic neighborhoods. Rural and suburban homes have less human traffic and may have less need for a routine cleansing and resealing process.

What we think about regularly influences our atmosphere. Total focus while cleansing is ideal; however, it takes years to develop that level of meditative skill. Even the best of us have our thoughts sometimes stray during a working, and where our thoughts go the magic will follow. Because of this, cleansing the home once or twice a month helps eliminate the ricochet effect of a spell having an unintended—or undesired—consequence. You can also control what lives in your home with you—particularly what may be of your own inadvertent creation. Your home will always have something living with you; you are never alone, but for the mighty amoeba. Yes, paranoiac, you are surrounded all the time. And that's a good thing: it keeps you humble, or at least amusingly twitchy. It also asserts your connection, molecule by molecule, to the rest of the world on all levels. You can't help being surrounded. But you can help what surrounds you, and that's where cleansing and house blessing comes in handy.

For any house (apartment, tent, dugout, dwelling) cleansing, apply the following principles:

1. Clutter = bad

2. Fire extinguishers and house insurance = good

3. Clear out the astral and physical first

4. After clearing out, then you cleanse

5. After cleansing, shield

6. After shielding, anchor

7. After anchoring, offer

8. After offering, invite your guests (and residents) and let them know the rules by verbalizing them clearly. Sometimes you may have to add consequences to your arrangement.

My typical house cleansing follows this process:

First I clear the clutter. I am a less than stellar housekeeper, so for me a clutter cleaning means taking clothes off the floor and books off the furniture. Once I have anything on the floor that might trip me moved out of the way, including any animal household members, I grab my broom and begin the process of cleansing everything.

The broom, or besom as some call it, is a ritual implement intended to sweep out stagnant and negative energies. I found my most recent besom in a Halloween costume shop, sold as a "real witches' broom." If it wasn't before, it is now. Starting at the most frequently used entrance to my home, I take the broom and begin to sweep, brushing particularly at corners, the ceiling, and behind walls. I also take the opportunity to disrupt any cobwebs in my way. Be very thorough on a first time cleansing: open the oven and microwave, sweep cupboards and closets, even brush over drains and electrical outlets (do the drains after the electrical outlets). Sometimes a rhyme or chant helps the magical flow of this process, such as "Out, about, I turn all out—what dawdles here, I turn out!"

Once the cleansing has been completed, the household should feel like it has more breathing room. The effect is temporary. A swept-through area left unattended fills again all too quickly. Nature abhors a vacuum. A shielding or warding must fill this void, or the void may be filled by something you don't want. You will get everything you swept out back, and often the sweep-outs bring their friends. Some people enjoy their homes being hotspots of chaotic energy. I don't, It has a detrimental (i.e. draining) effect on the inhabitants that pay the rent or mortgage, and most find it preferable to fill up the space with preselected energies and inhabitant that leave them their normal mental function.

I build protective energy in layers. I build the first layer by smudging my living space. I choose white sage because it suits the land I live on best; the ancestral spirits come from a culture that used sage, and respond best if I honor the traditions surrounding the plant. In order to smudge a home, I carry a lighter, a ceramic pot to catch the ashes, and the sage bundle. Sage frequently goes out when initially lit, so I carry the lighter to reignite it. I proceed through my home, waving the sage while holding the ceramic put beneath it, catching all ashes. Generally a brush through the corners and over the primary traffic areas establishes a strong, purified area. I visualize the sage spreading into every corner of the home, pushing through floors and ceilings, creating a glowing wall. Just so you're aware, sage has qualities that will cause you to sweat, and sweat profusely—and while a purge may be good for you and your skin, you might want to open some windows while you smudge.

A sweep and a smudge will hold for a bit, but if you're like me you'll want some assurance that your work will stick for a while. This is where shielding comes in. I prefer blessed water for my anchor. I mix a pinch of sea salt in with a cup of water, and I say a prayer that the salt and water be pure, and carry the blessings of water and earth.

It's acceptable to mix these ingredients in the bowl and then simply flick the water into corners, over doorways, and on windows. I store this material in a plastic spray bottle (pray 'n' spray) and spritz each room, door, and window in all the designated cleansing areas. The blessed water cleanses any residual energy that sweeping or smudging might have missed, and through the salt crystals in the water, give the sage something to anchor itself to. This strengthens the shield over the home by adding some reinforcements in the form of salt crystals.

Being of a religious bent, I always complete my house cleansing and warding with an offering to the gods of home and hearth. These beings are many, and cross many cultures. Because I incline toward the Hellenic mythos, I honor Hestia, but she is by no means the limits of domestic life. Other priests and priestesses I know opt for singular dedicated pantheons, often with strong arguments toward never playing mix 'n' match with gods.

In every pantheon I'm aware of, there is a feminine divinity that oversees the home. The Celtic Brigid is a popular domestic goddess frequently called upon, as is the Egyptian Hathor. Always do some research before asking for the blessing of any divinity, because what that divinity views as a blessing may not fit with your intentions. For instance, if you ask for the blessing of Pan, he may well bless you with some very literal fertility. Unplanned pregnancies are most certainly a double-edged sword of curse and blessing. Even something as seemingly innocuous as a house blessing can trigger deeper consequences whenever the gods are involved. Hit the library and read books with actual stories of the gods so you know what you're getting into before you open up the line and ask. These stories reveal plenty about the character of a given god or goddess, and they give strong clues of how to best approach them.

But you're not quite finished with house blessings and protections yet. You will likely need to ward once in a while, but it is not a task that needs repetition on a regular basis so long as your home is kept clean and stable. Warding puts a block on your home—a sort of sealant that doesn't allow any energies to pass in or out. This can create a new level of stagnation that can lead to an additionally unhealthy environment for living. Just like an organic being, the space you live in needs to be allowed to "breathe." A home shield allows for some traffic through the home—the shield simply filters out specific types of traffic you declare undesirable. Small amounts of astral traffic through the home are good things: if you call for assistance from the elements, or from local spirits, they can go through the shield because you invited them. Wards, however, tend to slow down the process because nothing gets through until you take the ward down.

Warding is best used in situations where there is a quantifiable physical threat to the safety of yourself or your home. Such instances include nearby thefts or robberies, a predatory criminal in your area, or a person directing threats clearly and unequivocally to you. Warding in no way replaces the need to call 911 should you wind up in a truly dangerous situation; however, it helps in delaying or preventing that need. Warding also helps in the extremely rare instances of hauntings or poltergeist activity.

In order to ward, you need to perform the basic house cleansing and blessing. Follow this with a self-purification; this may be a simple or complex action. I prefer simplicity in all things, so my purification follows this procedure: I lay out fresh clothes for myself, and after making sure the bathroom is clean, I draw myself a bath and add basic purifiers like sea salt and hyssop. The hyssop can be closed in a muslin bag or tea bag to prevent the hassle of having to fish it out of the drain afterwards. While in the bath, I pray to be cleansed of negativity, ill intention, and harmful relationships. As I pray, I submerge my head two or three times. Once I feel sufficiently purified, I drain the tub and dress in the clean clothing or robes I laid out for myself.

While dressed in clean clothing, I take some olive oil with a few drops of lemongrass essential oil mixed into it, or some specially blessed water, and walk to each door and window. At each entry to my home, I draw a simple pentagram or an equal armed cross—both are well known protective symbols. As I draw the symbol, I visualize it glowing until the light takes over the whole of my home. I make sure to ward all possible entrances: doors, windows, drains, outlets—even my cable modem. Any excess energies may no longer enter. While it's still possible to perform spells and rituals, the wards will have a deadening effect until they wear off. Any influence you invite through will feel muted through the filter of your wards.

If you're extra concerned for your safety, after warding your home you can do a simple protection spell for yourself. You can create a talisman such as a cross or a pentacle, or follow a simple candle spell for protection, such as that found in Ray Buckland's *Practical Candle Magic*. Think of these actions as additional backup to the normal precautions of locking your doors at night and making sure your cell phone has its emergency contacts clearly labeled.

These routine rituals establish your home as a sacred place. As most witches are their own priests and priestesses, their homes become their temples. Any temple requires routine cleansing and acknowledgment of its sacredness to be a fit temple. House cleansing, and sometimes warding, imprints that reminder on both yourself and on the traffic patterns of your home. This way you can ensure your home continues as both sacred place and sanctuary, where just entering fills you with peace and healing. Cleanse and bless regularly, and this feeling builds in strength over time.

A Gargoyle Guide

······

BY PATRICIA TELESCO

On many Victorian edifices, including churches, one can discover a gathering of winged creatures grinning down from their lofty perch as if to welcome or warn any visitor brave enough to approach. Somehow, these remnants of the Middle Ages became very popular architectural designs around the turn of the century and are still with us today. Where do they come from, and what do they represent?

The first gargoyles were actually medieval rainspouts. The name gargoyle comes from medieval French and means throat. These little beasts were both grotesque and humorous in construction, and adorned many lofty cathedrals.

To understand the use of gargoyles, we have to look to earlier cultures who often used fantastic, hideous faces to protect themselves from evil. Two examples of this are the gorgons of Greece and the image of the luck god Bes in Egypt. In both instances the ugly face was considered protective, as if negative spirits could be repelled by the ugly visages. Or they may be a representation of the human animal growling in the face of the unknowable, frequently frightening, spiritual realm.

These are just some of the rainspout images that can be found in some cities today:

Florentine: The watchdog-like gargoyle who sneers from its perch.

Tuscan: Popular on Italian towers, this is a chained gargoyle with incredible detail.

Lyons: A huge wingspan marks this gargoyle, as does the coat of arms on its chest. The Lyons carving is portrayed as dog-faced.

Notre Dame: There are several wonderful figures on this magnificent building that were later reproduced and used elsewhere. These include a winged, monkey-faced figure, a pointy-nosed dragon cornerstone, and a gargoyle who is cheerfully gnawing on a bone.

Griffins: Winged lions frequently seen on old-world castles.

Centaurs: Figures with the upper body of a man and lower body of a horse.

Cernunnos: Horned god of Pagan mythology.

Polycephali: Multi-headed gargoyles.

Hermaphrodites: Figures with both sexes represented in one body.

Sphinx: Right from the sands of Egypt, image of cunning and wisdom.

Hagodays: Creatures made into the form of Sanctuary door knockers, believed to have mystical powers of truth-seeing and protection.

The later part of this list illustrates that the early Christian church was very cunning. By channeling the Pagan images into decorative, useful items they were making a statement about the powers of the old court versus the new. These primal representations of our connection with the animal kingdom and nature thus become a fascinating note in ecclesiastical annals.

Glastonbury: The Common Ground of Avalon

......

BY DETRACI REGULA

Pagan gathering place? Mystic refuge? Christian church? Goddess worshipers haven? Few places on Earth combine the many worlds between the worlds as effectively as Glastonbury, and in this small town of 8,000 inhabitants, you never know who you will meet. It's a place of quests, where everyone desires to find a touch of another world. And they may well receive it.

Glastonbury lies on the Salisbury Plain, facing the sea in the south of England. Once an island itself, the rhythms of water are still flowing through it. Chalice Well, with its entwined Vesica Piscis ponds, and the compelling White Spring, which rises from the roots of Glastonbury Tor itself assure that the spiritual potency of water is never doubted here.

In the morning, before the crowds come, the destroyed remains of the Glastonbury Abbey are curiously peaceful and without stain. The Abbey was brutally suppressed by King Henry VIII, who had the then-abbot dragged to the Tor and hung; now, nature has reclaimed the gray stones and restored some peace. On one fragment, a dozen white birds nest; opposite, an equal number of black birds make the place home. At unlikely spots a bit of green clings to the wall itself.

Though Glastonbury has been troubled, it has purified itself. Walking through a Christian temple, ruined at the hands of other Christians, the visitor feels strangely at peace. "Henry has a lot to answer for," my companion, who had been completely uninterested in visiting Glastonbury, muttered as we wandered by the remains of the high arches.

It was hard to leave the Abbey, but the Tor beckoned, crowned with the Tower of St. Michael, saint in charge of suppressing dragons. This is all that remains of the church that once covered most of the top of the Tor. The air was clear, sunny, and "filled with sparkles" as Dion Fortune described a particularly memorable day on the Tor where she lived at Chalice Orchard. Although the Abbey is near the Tor, iron gates keep the two separate, maybe a bit of the magic keeping separate the fairy and the most recent faith. We walked the long way around the ground through the High Street and headed back toward the Tor, whose tower is strangely invisible even at closer rang, concealed by a subtle shift in ground level or a vigorous tree.

The other shift in ground quality was the incredible muddiness of the back way up the Tor, which we had been assured was shorter. And quicker. Rising up from a residential section of

Glastonbury, the way looked easy enough, until a dozen yards along when the mud was passing my ankles. We went around to the more commonly used way and discovered the White Spring. Its sound caught our attention first, a gentle gurgling under iron gratings at the side of the street. Following the water, we entered a room out of another world—a cave filled with a coffee house. More of the spring ran in narrow channels through the floor at our feet, and a magical shop nearby offered ritual blades whose hilts were masterfully carved with divine forms. Roots from the Tor hung down from the ceiling, and the lighting was largely by candlelight. Beyond the public areas other chambers skipped away into shadow. Once again it was hard to tear ourselves away, but the top of the Tor was still calling.

The path up the Tor went by Chalice Orchard, where a sign reminded gawkers that it was private property. This side of the Tor blessedly was not muddy, and the way up looked reassuringly simple. We had only a few hours to spend in Glastonbury, so the remains of the maze path, which takes several hours, were beyond us. The ascent was dizzying, and though I was in reasonably good shape, my heart was pounding and the air seemed thin. I looked at the Tower in the distance and thought, with the body betraying the spirit for a moment that perhaps this was close enough.

But now my companion had caught the glow of the Tor and, thrilled with the ascent, thundered on, offering a hand to me at moments. In the last stretch, we passed a group of dun-colored Hathorian cows that lay unexpectedly along the path, lowing. Then we were at the Tower, whose height induced vertigo when we looked up inside it. As Dion had said, the air was full of sparkles outside, and around us, England stretched out like a tablecloth.

Far away were the bell towers of Wells. Pastoral fields stretched in all directions, reminding us of the sea that once isolated this high hill, a flooded field shone glassy beneath the blue sky. The miraculously clear air changed as we watched, and a slight mist began emanating from the ground all around. As the sun descended, so did we. Someone began drumming in the Tower, and the thrilling sound reverberated through the Tor.

Or was it in the Tower? Glastonbury has its legends as a hollow mound reaching into the Under—or Other—World as well. You can never be sure what world you perceive at magical Glastonbury.

Ritual Breads

......

by Magenta Griffith

A large symbolically shaped bread is an excellent contribution to any seasonal ritual. My coven has used the bread god to symbolize John Barleycorn, the god of vegetation who rises every spring and is cut down every autumn to feed the people. We have also used Kore bread to celebrate spring for many years. Here's how to make these special breads.

The Bread God

2 packages of yeast or 2 tbsp. dry yeast

½ c. warm water (put a drop on your wrist to test; warm, but not too hot)

6 c. white flour *or* 3 c. white flour and 3 c. whole wheat flour

3 eggs beaten (reserve 1 tbsp. for glazing loaf)

3 to 4 tbsp. honey or sugar

3 tbsp. oil

1 tbsp. salt

1 c. milk or water

Extra flour

Hand mixing method: Dissolve yeast in warm water, allow to stand for 5 minutes to proof (test that the yeast works). Put flour in a large bowl, make a well in the center, and pour in the yeast mixture. In a separate bowl, mix the eggs and reserve one tablespoon for the glaze, if desired. Then add sweetener, oil, salt, and water, and mix, then add wet to dry and mix well. Turn out onto a lightly floured surface, flour your hands, and knead for 10 minutes. Add more flour if needed. Dough should not stick to the board, but it also should not dry out or become crumbly.

Electric mixer method: If you have a heavy-duty electric mixer with a dough hook, you can use this method. Dissolve yeast in warm water in mixing bowl and allow to stand for 5 minutes to proof. Mix the eggs together and reserve one tablespoon for the glaze, if desired. Add the eggs and rest of the liquids and sweetener, and mix using the dough hook. Add salt, then flour one cup at a time as quickly as possible to avoid overkneading. Add up to one cup more flour, a tablespoon at a time if needed to keep dough from sticking to the bowl. Knead about ten minutes.

Both methods: Place the dough in an oiled bowl, cover, and let rise in a warm place for one hour until doubled in bulk. Punch down and knead for one minute. Now comes the shaping of the bread god, somewhat like working with Play-Doh.

For this, turn out the dough onto the floured surface. To make one very large figure, divide the dough into three parts. To make smaller figures, divide the dough in half, then into thirds, and go through this process twice to form two figures. Roll each piece of dough between your hands into long ropes. Lay these parallel on the surface.

Leave some length at each end and braid the middle into the body. Use the three strands at one end to shape the arms and head, on the other end to the legs and either a phallus or vulva. You can use dried fruit for eyes, nipples, or other details. Be creative.

Baking: Place the bread god on a baking sheet that has been greased and dusted with corn meal and allow the bread to rise uncovered in a warm place. If you are forming it into one large bread god, you may not have a big enough sheet. In this case, you can overlap two baking sheets, being careful to always move them as one.

Allow the bread god to double in size, which will take about one hour. Twenty minutes before baking time, preheat the oven to 350 degrees F.

Before you bake, mix the reserved tablespoon of egg and one tablespoon of water and use this mixture to glaze the loaf. You may also sprinkle poppy seeds or sesame seeds on strategic places if you want the effect of hair on the god's head, beard, crotch, or chest. Bake 35 to 40 minutes, or until the bread god is nicely browned and sounds hollow when tapped. If you have a hot oven, check after 30 minutes.

Carefully transfer the bread god to a wire rack and cool. If you have used two sheets, be especially careful when removing it from the oven.

This is a versatile dough. Feel free to experiment with other shapes, like a sun wheel or a spiral, as well as the traditional braided loaf. In this last case, simply divide into three parts, roll into ropes, and braid as you would hair. Don't be afraid to be creative.

Low Fat, Low Cholesterol Variation

You can eliminate the eggs in the above recipe. Simply increase the liquid to 1½ cups. I would advise using low fat or skim milk in this case rather than water. The oil can be decreased to 2 tablespoons, but the bread needs oil in it. You can use milk to glaze the unbaked loaf, or you can leave it unglazed.

Kore Bread

This recipe is a variation of a Russian bread made in the spring, usually for Easter. The abundance of eggs is both practical and symbolic. The egg is a symbol of everlasting life, of life renewed, and of new life yet to come.

Also, hens start laying more eggs as the days get longer, so in the spring, farmers have more eggs than they know what to do with.

1 c. water

½ stick cinnamon

4 whole cloves

4 allspice berries

1 bay leaf

10 to 12 coriander seeds

Mix ingredients in a pan, bring to a boil and boil for 5 minutes. Strain, set aside, and allow to cool.

In a sauce pan, scald 1 cup milk, add 1 cup butter, then cool the mixture to room temperature. In a bowl, dissolve 4 tablespoons dry yeast and 1 tablespoon honey in 1 cup warm water, and set aside to proof for five minutes.

10 to 12 c. flour

1 tbsp. salt

1½ c. honey

2 tsp. anise oil

Peel of 1 orange, grated

10 eggs

Mix flour and salt in a large bowl, add dissolved yeast, honey, milk mixture, anise oil, orange peel, and spiced water. Mix in a heavy-duty electric mixer with a dough hook for 15 minutes, adding eggs one at a time. Remove from the mixer and add the rest of the flour with a spoon, turning onto a floured surface and kneading in the last of it until you have a soft dough.

Put the dough into a buttered bowl, cover, and let rise until doubled in size, about 1 hour. Punch down, let double again, punch down again, and let double in size a third time.

Turn onto a floured surface and knead briefly. Divide the dough in two, then divide each half into thirds. Let the dough rest under a towel for 10 minutes.

Roll three pieces of dough into 24-inch strands. Braid these together, then join the ends to form a kind of wreath. Transfer to a well-greased cookie sheet, and repeat with the rest of the dough. Cover the dough and let rise until doubled, about 1 hour.

Gently push 4 dyed eggs deeply into the quarters of each wreath, and if you'd like, put one in the center of each. I like to use naturally dyed eggs. To do this, place eggs in a pan of water with the skins of several yellow or purple onions. Boil the water to produce a pleasant reddish brown or purplish red color, respectively. You can also use a heaping tablespoon of turmeric to produce yellow eggs (use a metal pot; turmeric is a permanent dye). The eggs must be pushed deeply into the dough so the baking won't force them out.

Beat together 2 eggs and 1 tablespoon milk and brush the surface of the loaves with this mixture, avoiding the eggs. Sprinkle generously with sesame seeds.

Bake in a preheated 350 degree F oven for about 1 hour until done. The crust should be golden and the bread should sound hollow when tapped. Gently remove the bread from the pans and cool on a wire rack.

Makes two large braided loaves. You can make a half-recipe for one loaf, but it's almost as much work for one as for two.

For Further Study

Beard on Bread. James Beard. Knopf, 1995.

Bread Winners. Mel London. Rodale Press, 1979.

Some Magical Recipes

......

by Patricia Telesco

To help get your cookbook started, here are some recipes to which all kinds of wonderful magic can be added.

Bread Pudding (Winter)

Winter was often hard for the farmer, so the staple of the farm family was bread, which required few costly ingredients. It was considered ill fortune to burn or throw away bread. Instead the leftover bits were either given to the animals or made into this tasty treat.

  2 c. candied fruit

  1 c. sliced almonds (or other favorite nuts)

  ½ loaf thinly sliced bread

  ½ stick butter or margarine

2 eggs

½ c. milk

¼ tsp. nutmeg

½ tsp. cinnamon

Mix together candied fruit, almonds, and bread. Grease a bread pan well. Next, layer the mixture in the bread pan with dabs of butter between each layer. When the pan is full or the ingredients are exhausted, prepare a mixture of well-beaten eggs, milk, and spices. Pour this over the layered bread and bake in the oven at 350 degrees F for about 30 minutes or until golden brown.

Magical Affiliations: luck, kinship, sustenance through hard times

Flower Salad (Spring)

All around nature is blooming, so why not celebrate its color with a salad of fresh petals? Many flowers, besides having natural magical associations, are edible. The only caution here is to rinse your petals in cool water to remove any garden debris.

Mix together ½ cup each: gladiolus, carnations, dried chrysanthemums (crushed for garnish), nasturtiums, roses, tulips, and violets.

Change proportions to personal pleasure, color significance, and general beauty. Dressing may be herbed vinaigrette, yogurt, or a bit of sweet cream.

Magical Affiliations: growth, improved creative energy, new endeavors, romance, simple pleasures, inner loveliness

Pink Dandelion Wine (Summer)

This is a think ahead recipe as it takes one year to age properly. During summer months when those pesky dandelions are plaguing the lawn, smile graciously, pluck them (thanking the earth), and make some ritual wine for next year!

2 qts. dandelion blossoms

2 qts. water

1 lemon

2 c. fresh or frozen raspberries

¼ tsp. cinnamon

4 to 5 c. sugar

⅓ cake active yeast (or wine yeast)

Take the blossoms, remove stems and leaves, and boil in water. Remove from the heat and let stand overnight, then strain. Then add lemon, raspberries, cinnamon, and sugar (so it is overly sweet to the taste). Warm mixture over low flame until the sugar is dissolved (honey may be substituted in equal proportions).

Next, when the mixture is lukewarm, add active yeast that has been suspended in warm water. Cover the pan with a towel and let it sit for three days undisturbed. As you check it, visualize the energy in your wine increasing even as the bubbles are forming (a sign of fermentation starting).

Finally, strain the mixture again and bottle in loosely corked bottles. Once the corks no longer pop out, taste to see if the wine needs any additional sugar. If so, return it to the stove and sweeten to taste, but bring it to a boil so as to kill the yeast. Cork tightly and let age for one year in a cool, dark area for best results.

Magical Affiliations: creativity, god energy, increasing power, psychic attunement, love

Potato Pie (Fall)

Potatoes are a primary food item in American households because of their durability in harsh conditions and long shelf life.

¼ lb. mashed potatoes

1 qt. milk

½ stick butter

4 eggs

¼ tsp. salt (optional)

¼ tsp. pepper (optional)

½ tsp. garlic (fresh minced)

1 cup grated Parmesan cheese

Place mashed potatoes in a large bowl. Blend in milk, butter, eggs, salt, pepper, garlic, and Parmesan cheese and mix thoroughly. Put mixture into a greased baking pan and bake at 325 degrees F until fluffy and ginger colored.

Add for magical significance: meats (for prosperity or grounding), sharp cheese (for protection), and broccoli and/ or cauliflower (for growth or foundations).

Magical Affiliations: endurance or strength, benevolence and sharing, thankfulness

Natural Remedies for Wintertime Ailments

......

by Edain McCoy

While no natural remedy should replace the advice and care of a qualified doctor, there are numerous medicines to be found in nature that can help see us through the aches, pains, and chills of winter's colds and flus. Of course, the best medicine is always prevention. The herbs bearberry and garlic have proven themselves to be excellent tonics for the immune system when taken regularly, and are particularly good for helping to make you "cold resistant."

Soup to Help Loosen Congestion

This soup packs a spicy punch, but usually does the trick without resorting to drugs. Purists, please note that the basic ingredient is chicken stock, which has proven to help treat colds.

16 oz. chicken broth

1 minced red onion

⅛ to ¼ tsp. cayenne pepper

1 tsp. dried boneset

1 tsp. dried chamomile

¼ tsp. black pepper

¼ tsp. garlic powder

⅛ tsp. sage

Salt to taste

Set all ingredients in a large stockpot to gently boil. Serve steaming hot.

Fever-Reducing Tea

Many herbs contain anti-inflammatory properties and have been used successfully to help reduce fevers and ease aches and pains. A fever can be a sign of serious illness, and children under twelve or anyone with a fever that persists for more than two days or goes over 104 degrees F should be taken to a doctor. This recipe makes about six cups. It can be kept in the refrigerator for up to three days. It reheats well in the microwave or over the stove.

1½ tbsp. black willow bark (omit if you are
   allergic to aspirin)

1½ tbsp. black elder (increase to 2 tbsp. if you
   are omitting the willow bark)

1 tsp. blessed thistle

½ tbsp. goldenseal

2 tsp. echinacea

½ tbsp. linden flowers

1½ tsp. chamomile

Place the ingredients in a cheesecloth or large tea ball. Tie
up the cloth or secure the tea ball and place it into 6½ cups of
boiled water. Allow it to steep for at least 10 minutes. This tea
makes no claim to begin the best tasting brew ever created, but
it works well. You may add sugar, honey, or rice syrup if you
wish. Take one cup every four to six hours as needed.

Natural Cough Suppressant

Using the well-known honey and lemon as a base, this thick paste
contains the mild narcotic of bugleweed, a similar property to
the chemical codeine, which is often prescribed to treat severe
coughs. Dry coughs can be treated every four hours. Coughs that
are bringing up phlegm should be left alone until bedtime because they are beneficial in purging the illness from your body. In
a large bowl thoroughly mix:

1 lb. honey

1½ c. lemon juice (avoid oil-based substitutes)

½ tbsp. bugleweed

½ tbsp. coltsfoot

8 oz. unsweetened cherries, crushed

This will keep in the refrigerator for about a week. Use 2 to 3 tablespoons every four hours as needed.

Anti-Diarrheal Preparation

While it is usually best to let diarrhea run its course so that whatever is making you sick can escape, there are times when we simply must pull ourselves together and get out of the bathroom. The following recipe is high in vitamin C and healthy bacteria, which can put you back on track without the artificial chemicals found in over-the-counter preparations. In a large bowl mix:

1½ c. blackberries, crushed

½ c. raspberries or black cherries, crushed

½ c. strained carrots (the baby food variety is perfect)

½ lb. acidophilus yogurt

2 sliced bananas

⅛ tsp. nutmeg

¼ tsp. ginger

½ c. cooked rice, cooled (optional)

Chill and eat. This preparation is tasty enough that you won't feel like you're taking your medicine. Eat as much as you like, but don't overdo. The unused portion must be covered and refrigerated.

Wilderness Magic

......

by Kenneth Johnson

There is a wonderful passage in one of the old epics of King Arthur. It says that whenever the knights began their quest for the grail, they plunged straight into the wilderness where the woods are thickest.

Clever knights. They knew where to find the magic.

But then perhaps they were not so clever. After all, don't most of our European fairy tales begin in much the same way? The tree spirit, the elvish helper, the old witch, or the magic fountain—all are discovered when the heroine or hero of the story wanders away from the well-ordered village, the peaceful town, the easy and well-marked path, and enters the wilderness. Perhaps it was simply common knowledge back then that the primal chaos of trees, rocks, and water was the most potent and magical energy source available.

In many, if not most, magical and folk traditions, the world is the body of the Earth Mother herself. It is no wonder then that the trees that constitute her beautiful hair and the rocks that constitute her strong bones are the source of so much magic. Whoever we may be, of whatever cultural origin, all our ancestors were tribal at one time or another, and hence they all lived close to the magic. Wherever we now live, wilderness is generally not that far away—perhaps in the closest state park or forest area. And there are many ways you can touch the magic of the wilderness for yourself.

First, like most traditional peoples the world over, pre-Christian Europeans seem to have believed that the center of shamanic power lay in our midsection—between the lower diaphragm and the middle belly. Once you are in the woods, focus your attention on this spot on your body. Don't worry too much about its exact location. It's a little different for everyone. Your body will find it for you if you simply focus on seeking a primal source of internal energy. Keep your awareness there, as if it's the actual center of your being.

Once you have done this, you will find that the paths of energy in the earth itself just seem to pull you along. When you're really focused, you will be aware of zones of power in the earth. When you've found such a place of power, there are a number of things you can do.

First, you can work with the rocks. Most rocks, whether tiny stones or great boulders, have a "soft spot" somewhere, which allows you to enter into them in the spirit. Use your intuition, eyes, and a sense of touch to find that spot. Then, meditatively, go inside. Many people report seeing visions of long ago—the very past of Earth itself. The whole record of Mother Earth's experience is stored inside her bones, the rocks. If there is a stream or a lake, you have a wonderful place to get rid of some of your emotional baggage. In European folk songs, sad lovers are always sitting by the banks of a lake or river. Why? Because it is believed that water purifies our sexual selves and washes away negativity. Give your sorrows to the water and meditatively feel them slip away from you forever.

If there are plenty of trees, you may be able to locate one that "likes" you. I'm not joking. Place your back against a tree so it can feel your aura. If it likes you, you will know. Then you can become one with the tree. Feel its essence go into your center of power. Then open your eyes. If you are lucky, you will be able to see the world through the tree's eyes. Believe me, when this works its better than any psychedelic.

Finally, you can simply dance. That's right. There's no particular reason to sit still in a place of power. You might as well just dance, moving to your own inner music and the music of the sun and the wind. The rocks and trees will enjoy it.

A Wad of Lint:
Thoughts on Magical Tools

......

by Jim Garrison

I can't help but listen to the voice of the rain, which is not here yet. In my head a thunderstorm rages; outside it's a relatively quiet night, so far. I like the rain. It's cleansing and healing, sweet and cold like the touch of happy tears in the night. I usually go running in the rain. That's how I caught pneumonia a couple times.

Ground and center. I pull the elements through my heart and the dance begins. I do not own an altar, so I use the floor. I have no robes, so I stand naked in the moonlight. I forego all the tools one is taught to use in the craft, and instead rely upon the gifts of my ancestors and the gods. I dance the circle with my bare feet and my empty hands. My voice fills the space with chants brought to me by my imagination; gifts of the muse, these words and sounds mean more to the deeper me than any book. The quarters spill into the circle by my invitation, my fingers and fist moving with the dance and performing patterns of movement that open the doorways to beyond. I can taste the breeze of the ghost woods. I'm home.

The body is your first altar, and the most important one you'll ever get in this life, or any other. Take proper care of your body, this is where your spirit resides and it is the living legacy of your ancestors. Our blood carries the memories of the old ones of our lineages all the way back to the time when we were all children of the first dream.

The heart is the first and most powerful drum anyone ever learns to dance to. It takes more effort, for some, but it's the chord around which you are arranged, the underlying beat of your spiritual rhythm, which is as unique as anyone else's.

Your first tools are your hands and feet. Learning to move is not so easy. It's generally considered to be self-explanatory, something you just do. Most of us need to learn how to really move. Dancing is one of the oldest forms of achieving ecstatic states, and a very powerful means to work magic.

It's not the athame or the wand that scribes the circle, it's you. Tools act as lenses for the energies you are working with, or they are symbols for causing responses deep within yourself. With discipline and visualization, people can do everything a tool is used for with their own hands, at least as far as casting circles and spellcraft are concerned.

You do not own the words; they are given to you. Following a tradition doesn't mean that you have to enslave yourself to another person's spiritual vision. Find the means to make the words meaningful for you. The muse will dance with you and give you the words you need if you but ask her.

With mirth and reverence we can dance in the moonlight with the ancestors and learn the secret names of things as yet unborn, see the patterns of life and death move through us like fluctuating tides. There are no outside things, no objects of power or talisman that you must have to practice magic.

Between the world and beyond is the abyss, and there is nothing there except what you bring within yourself.

Eliminating the trappings, and returning to the Spartan simplicity and purity of working without your tools and preconceived notions is refreshing, a challenge of your abilities that quickly tells you if you've gotten to rely upon the props too much. It opens up new pathways you might not have seen otherwise; you've stepped outside of the usual limitations and everything is new and wild again.

Magical Stones
and Your Sun Sign

......

by Kim Rogers-Gallagher

Over many years of being an astrologer, I've found that certain stones possess energies that seem tailor-made for use by each of the sun signs. So if you're feeling the need to increase your personal power or bring out the most positive qualities of your sign, take a look at this list and try the stones I've mentioned. No matter what you use, keep in mind that carrying or wearing any stone on the right means you're projecting or sending out that energy, while using it on the left means you're filtering what you receive or attract from your environment.

Aries

Red belongs to Mars, your ruling planet, so you'll love blood-stones, rubies, and garnets, which are all good fiery choices. When you'd like to tamp your fire down a bit, try carnelian. It promotes peace, harmony, and patience, but holds fire and lends a warrior-energy to the wearer. Now, your traditional birthstone is the diamond—not a bad fit since diamonds are known for purity, and Aries energy is pure, too—clean and uncluttered by hidden motives. If your budget doesn't allow for jeweler's diamonds, substitute Herkimer diamonds, long used as a stand-in.

Taurus

There's nothing you like more than a great big chunk of polished, perfect rock of any kind. The stones that are best for you are lapis, that gorgeous blue stone that's laced with flecks of gold, and rich, fertile jade. The emerald is your traditional birthstone. Emeralds are the charming representative of both the earth element and the planet Venus—the building blocks you are made of. Its soothing color suits you since you're spring-born. This stone is most power-ful when set in copper, the metal that corresponds with Venus.

Gemini

Since you so love variety, it's no wonder your birthstone is the agate. The agate is also associated with Mercury, your ruling planet. It's an aid to truth-telling and good to carry when you want your words to be accurate. Although fluorite is not tradi-tionally associated with Gemini, it's a natural match. Fluorite is connected to the air element, as it keeps the mind keen. Stick it on the computer and pick it up when you get stuck between paragraphs.

Cancer

Your planet is the moon, so the moonstone is naturally connected to you. Its gentle energy protects against absorbing the emotions of others. Sapphires have an affinity with the moon, too, and will magnify your natural instinct and psychic powers. Chalcedony (a translucent, milky quartz) calms the emotions, and, like moonstones, will keep away depression and sadness—quite a boon for an emotional creature like you. Any pink stone with soothing properties, like rose quartz or rhodochrosite, is also a good talisman for Cancer. Carry or wear any stone on your left (the "incoming side") as a filter for the emotions.

Leo

Like Aries, a kindred fire sign, you love red, so when it comes to gems and stones, the royal ruby springs to mind. Speaking of royalty, have whatever you wear set in that most royal of all metals—gold. Nothing suits a legend more, and gold has a long-standing link with the sun, your ruling planet. To increase your natural courage and help you speak eloquently, a trait any performer appreciates, wear carnelian. Amber is also a good match for you, as it holds the life force your sign is famous for.

Virgo

Although the agate is one of your birthstones, the type that seems to correspond best with you is the moss agate, a lovely clear stone with feathery green threads running through it that look like ferns. This stone is best worn while gardening, one of your very favorite pastimes. Agates also promote good physical health, and health is your business, after all. Your other birthstone, the aventurine, increases the perceptive powers, sharpens the intellectual faculties, and helps to fine-tune the eyesight—something that any craftsperson can use.

Libra

Your traditional birthstone is the opal, but there are other stones that can be worn or carried to help you achieve your goal of finding and keeping that one special other. Any stone associated with Venus, your ruling planet, will do nicely, such as lapis lazuli. This lovely blue stone with golden flecks of pyrite mystically blends the energies of Venus and Mars (the planets in charge of relationships), and is worn to soothe, heal, and calm the wearer. Another good stone for Libra is kunzite, since its specialty is attracting love.

Scorpio

Black is Pluto's color, and red belongs to Mars, the planet that ruled Scorpio before Pluto was discovered. These are the traditional power colors, and power is your specialty—so these stones will attract you most. Red stones like carnelian, jasper, and red garnets appeal to your warrior side, and black stones fascinate you—like apache tears, black tourmaline, or hematite. To ground and protect yourself, use Pluto's favorite stones—spinel, kunzite, or rutilated quartz, which is perfect for Scorpio since it's a stone within a stone, and, like you, is full of buried treasure.

Sagittarius

Sagittarius's most important goal is to truly be a "wise one," so sodalite is wonderful for you. It helps to gain wisdom and to pass that wisdom back out into the world. Sodalite (and sugilite) also calms the mind and may help even Sagittarians settle down long enough to meditate. Amethyst, ruled by Sag's planet, Jupiter, is another good match. It clears the mind and quickens the wit. You'll love both blue and amber topaz, too, said to bring wealth and happiness to all December-born.

Capricorn

Rock endures, and permanence is a quality Capricorn finds all too rare, so you're quite fond of all stones. Most books say darker stones are your favorites, like onyx, hematite, and obsidian, because they're affiliated with Saturn, your planet, but try malachite. It operates like a magnet when it comes to attracting a good deal, and if you carry this stone on your left, you'll draw business success. Malachite also helps heal broken bones, and since your sign rules the skeleton of the body, the stone is a kindred spirit.

Aquarius

Although your birthstone is the gentle, peace-loving amethyst, your energies seem to blend better with stones that conduct ideas, since you're an air sign, and communication is your business. Aventurine is carried to enhance mental clarity and keenness, and sphere, a greenish stone, is reputed to help with processing information. The best conductor of all is clear quartz, however, so it's not surprising to find clusters placed strategically throughout an Aquarian's home—especially around the computer.

Pisces

The color of any stone you carry directly affects your disposition. So if you're feeling like you need to put out a little more energy than you've got, toss a couple of red stones into your right (or "outgoing" side) pocket. Red carried there gives our personal presentation a fiery "lift." As far as birthstones go, the amethyst has always been yours, and appropriately so: these gentle lavender crystals lift the spirits and protect you from addictions, and they aid in good judgment. Sugilite has also been used, just lately, as a birthstone for Pisces. It's a relatively new stone, but it seems to bestow psychic awareness and is said to make the wearer wise.

Growing Your Own Crystals

......

by Forte Robins

In every magical supply shop there are displays of crystals and semi-precious stones. If you've ever worked with crystals, you know how useful they can be, and you may be aware that some of the crystals available for purchase in stores are man-made. What you may not realize is the crystal-growing process can be done in your own kitchen. Crystal-growing kits are available in museums, and hobby and educational toy stores. The kits are designed to grow different crystal shapes, as the packaging will show you.

Why grow your own crystals? Besides being fun, crystal growing provides you with an extremely personal and flexible magical tool. A basic magic principle states that any item you create or shape is going to conduct your energy better than a impersonal item. Crystal growing gives you an opportunity to shape the creation of what is normally Earth's most solid and permanent of icons.

There is a difference, however, in the crystals you will be growing, and the naturally occurring variety. While the shape is the same, the chemical composition is different. Crystals, both the man-made and the natural ones, are formed by a tight and well-organized molecular structure. It is that structure, in addition to the chemical composition, that gives the diamond its famous hardness, and makes it such an ideal tool for focusing energy. Man-made crystals are used in lasers, watches, and computers because of their energy-focusing capabilities. Crystalline structure not only focuses power well, it is an excellent storage medium for your energy.

The instructions in crystal-growing kits are not difficult to follow, but may take some experimentation to master. The tools required in addition to the kits are readily available. For example, you will need an old saucepan and a food scale. You will also need a quiet place to leave the growing vessels, as they must remain undisturbed while the crystals are forming. The crystals are grown by dissolving the kit's chemical solution in an exact amount of hot water. Hot water will hold more of the chemical than cold water, so as the solution cools in the growing vessels, the chemicals will be forced out of the cooling water and become solid. This also happens as the water evaporates. Because of the shape of the molecules that make the chemicals, when they become solid, they will naturally form crystals.

The growth takes several days, and in itself can be done as a ritual. I grow mine on the waxing moon, projecting my energy into the growing vessels every night. As with any item you are charging, remember not to project energy if you are tired or angry. In the case of an already formed object, what you put in will be what you get out, but in the case of item creation, what you put in will affect the very nature of the created item.

So what can you do with your crystals? Anything you can do with a normal crystal and more. Because you are charging them as they grow, you can attune them to a goal as they are forming. Imaging divining with a clear crystal you grew solely for that purpose! The attunement can be as complicated or simple as you like using whatever correspondences you feel are appropriate. For example, you might project energy into a divination crystal only at night, leaving the vessels where moonlight can fall on them, and cover the window during the day. To aid in attuning your projected energy towards divination, you might drink eye-bright tea, or while you project energy, burn incense that will aid in divination such as nutmeg, lilac, or bistort. On the other hand, if you desire green crystals to use for healing spells, think the water/ chemical solution with a small amount of green food coloring and consecrate the solution to the purpose of healing. Empower healing crystals during the day, and visualize your energy coming from your hands as vivid green light. You might also want to cover the growing vessels with sheer green cloth or cellophane so the crystals can absorb the power of the colored light as well.

Your crystals will also work in the deceptively simple role of power batteries. When you need extra energy for a ritual (such as during the waning moon), place a number of your crystals around you at the beginning of the ritual. Visualize the points shooting beams of pure energy into you. Or place the points toward an item you wish empowered, instruct the crystals to release their energy into the item, and visualize laser-like beams performing the charge.

It is important to note that your crystals, having a different chemical composition than naturally occurring crystals, are water-soluble. This means you can't wash them, and it's not a good idea to put them in your mouth. It does, however, provide you with another way to use them. The growing process will create a few large specimens, but also a quantity of smaller pieces. Those small bits are hard to handle, but contain your energy just as the large ones do. One way to release that energy is to leave them in a bowl filled with water. The water will dissolve the crystal bits, just as a running river will wear down a mountain. As the water does its work, your energy will be released into the air to empower your spell. (Note that if you used food coloring, it will be released as well, and might stain the bowl. In any case, you shouldn't later use the same bowl for eating.)

These small crystals can also be placed into small decorative jars and then used as focal points for a spell. Runes can be drawn on the jar, herbs can be added, etc. In addition to the normal power of the spell, you'll be getting the energy the crystals absorbed while growing. Or since oil will not dissolve your crystals, try dropping a point or two into your essential oil bottles to give the oil an extra punch.

The biggest drawback of homegrown crystals is their temporary nature. While is it true that being involved in the creation of an item personalizes it, it is also true that things done quickly don't have the staying power conveyed by slow growth. Your crystals will not last as long as those Mother Nature worked on for thousands of years. However, if you keep them away from water, they will last indefinitely until used. The trick here is to experiment and follow your intuition. Have fun, and blessed be!

The Elements of Spells

......

by Ember Grant

When creating your own spells you are limited only by your imagination. The correspondences and styles for spellwork are many: colors, elements, candles, stones, and herbs are just a few of the items you can use in spells.

Many people prefer simple spells such as candle magic, but blending this with other items can provide new and energized spells. This article concerns working with the four basic elements: earth, air, fire, and water. Combining them with your usual spell items allows for even more creative opportunities and will result in a more original and personal spell.

One method that words well is to create a spell jar, which expands on candle magic. To do this, partially fill a glass container with water and add stones or shells and sprinkle the appropriate herbs on the water. Dress a candle with oil that corresponds to your magical working and carve an appropriate symbol into it, then float it in the water. It goes without saying that these things are best done while visualizing your intent and within a magic circle. The spell jar provides an environment for combining all the elements: earth, air, fire, and water. When the candle has burned out, reuse its wax, keep the stones, and return the water and herbs to the earth.

Of course, you may still tailor your spell around a specific element depending on the nature of your need. One method for earth-centered spells is to mix stones, herbs, and nuts with earth and place a candle or draw a rune in a pile of this stuff while visualizing your intent. For a water-oriented spell, use sand and shells. When the spell is complete, simply return the items to the ground or sea. Save the candle wax if you can. This can be melted down and reused to make new candles.

Feathers are good to use in air spells. Place very small ones in sachets or pillows; mix with earth and sand mixtures; float on water; or anoint with a drop of oil and release in a strong wind. You may also create a bundle of feathers, herbs, and flowers then tie with a ribbon. The ribbon can be decorated with runes and oils and be of a corresponding color.

Depending on the other elements you would like to combine, float the bundle on the water, bury in the ground, or burn it. Watch for natural items wherever you go. Look around for feathers, nuts, fallen leaves, rocks, shells, pinecones, sand, and water, especially in public areas such as beaches and parks; though always be sure you do not remove items from a protected area. Alternately, you can buy some of these items in stores or order them via a mail-order source. But certainly it's more exciting and energizing if you can find them yourself in nature. Remember to take only what you will need for the moment and never dig up an entire plant.

However, harvesting a few seeds of the plant in the fall will allow you to grow it yourself. Collect just a jar of sand, a small bottle of water, a couple of leaves, or rocks—and give thanks to the land as you do so. Grow your own herbs if you can, even the smallest patio or balcony can support a few containers of plants. These add to the power of the herbs in your spells and assure they are grown in conditions you can monitor and keep organic.

Be creative! If you pour your own candles, mix stones or shells in the wax. Being unique ensures variety and personal energy in all your spells. Happy spell-weaving!

THE NINE SACRED TREES

......

BY LILY GARDNER

Most famous among tree worshipers were the Druids who worshiped in the sacred groves of Great Britain. They gathered the branches and fruit of their sacred trees to fashion besoms, staffs, wands, and amulets. Nine species of tree were observed as having magical properties: birch, rowan, ash, alder, willow, hawthorn, oak, hazel, and holly.

Birch

Tall and slender with white bark and silvery leaves, the birch is the most graceful tree on earth. Birch is the tree with which to contact the world of spirits. The dead were said to wear birch bark clothing in many tales of spirit visitation.

The birch tree also signifies new beginnings. Birch branches are often used for making wands, because the wand, signifying will, is what drives new projects. Shamans also use a hoop made of birch wood for shapeshifting. Birch twigs are gathered together for the brush of the besom, the female aspect of the witch's broom.

Tying a red ribbon around a birch branch will ward off the evil eye. Birch is also known for its protection. Cradles made from birch wood are believed to protect a sleeping baby, and birch twigs set in the rafters protect the house from lightning strikes.

Rowan

Rowan, or "witch tree," is the tree most loved by witches and fairies. Also known as mountain ash, delight of the eye, quickbeam, and whitty tree, rowan is most known for its protective properties. Fortunate is the householder who has a rowan tree planted near his home, for it is said that the rowan will protect the family from fire, theft, and disease. Two twigs of rowan tied in a simple cross with red thread are often hung over the door of a house or barn for good luck. The Scots often carry these crosses in their pockets or sewn into their clothing when they travel.

The rowan's red berries are sometimes strung into necklaces for good luck. Rowan, with its centuries-old association with witchcraft, is an excellent choice for spell work.

Alder

Alder is sometimes known as the king of the waters because it typically grows near lakes or streams. Its association with water makes it a powerful aid in divination, oracles, and healing. Italian witches combine alder sap with madder plant to produce a red dye for protective cords and ribbon.

Willow

As the alder is known as the king of the waters, the willow is queen. Willow magic is fertility magic. It binds the feminine birch twigs to the male handle of the besom. A very old custom is to place willow branches in the beds of barren women to encourage fertility.

Wands made of willow invoke the muses. Sacred to poets, the music of the wind through willow leaves provokes inspiration. Orpheus, the most famous of Greek poets, gained his gift of eloquence by carrying willow branches as he journeyed through the underworld. To help with dream work, place a willow twig underneath your pillow.

The weeping willow is associated with grief, especially as it relates to abandonment. A practice that continued for centuries for was for jilted lovers to wear willow hats. Willow trees often decorated gravestones; a willow planted on the grave was said to ease the passage of the departed.

Ash

Tall and strong, ash wood is prized for building and firewood. Like many of the sacred trees, all parts of the ash are used for magic. The wood of the ash tree is used for staffs; its seed pods, called "ash keys," are used for protection, and its leaves are used for love charms.

Ash is used as the phallic handle of the besom. After a couple is married, they "jump the broom" to ensure fertility. Perhaps this association with fertility has something to do with its leaves being used in love charms. Carrying ash leaves in your pocket will attract a lover to you.

A staff carved from ash is often hung over the threshold of a home for protection. An equal-armed cross carved from its wood will prevent a traveler from drowning. The only thing the ash will not protect you from is a storm. It is said that the ash tree attracts lightning.

Burning ash wood in your Yule fire will bring prosperity to the household for the year.

Hawthorn

Hawthorn is the principal tree used at Beltane and is known for its power to grant fertility. Witches who wash their faces from morning dew from the hawthorn on Beltane will be beautiful throughout the year.

> *The fair maid who*
> *The first of May*
> *Goes to the field at the break of day*
> *And washes in the dew*
> *From the Hawthorn tree*
> *Will ever after handsome be.*
> *—MOTHER GOOSE*

Wearing an amulet made from hawthorn wards off depression and restores happiness. Travelers, when coming upon a hawthorn tree, may wish to tear off a piece of their clothing to hang on the tree as a "wish rag." To do so ensures their wishes will come true.

Oak

The oak tree is associated with the Summer Solstice and the light half of the year. One of the oldest dramas in western Europe is the battle between the Oak King and the Holly King, which takes place during each solstice. The Oak King defeats the Holly King at the Winter Solstice, and sunlight begins to return to the north lands. On the Summer Solstice, the Oak King is defeated and the sun begins to decline.

Carrying a small piece of oak as an amulet protects the wearer. An equal-armed cross, made from oak twigs and tied with a red thread, will protect one's home from fire, theft, and illness. Acorns on the windowsill protect the house from lightning, and an oak fire draws away illness from the household. Catching a falling oak leaf midair will bring good fortune.

Hazel

As oak is known for its strength, hazel is known for its wisdom. The salmon of wisdom, from Celtic myth, gained his insight by swallowing nine hazelnuts.

Hazel is probably even better known as the wood used in dowsing sticks. The dowser uses a forked hazel stick that will point to where there is underground water. Before the seventeenth century, dowsing sticks were used to find both treasure and criminals.

Hazel's ability to find what is hidden makes it the perfect wood for divination. By eating hazelnuts before you practice any form of divination, you will enhance your reading. The nuts themselves are used in an old love charm performed on Samhain night. Place two hazelnuts side by side in the fire as you chant: *"If you love me, pop and fly! If you hate me, burn and die."*

Crowns of hazel twigs are called wishing caps. When worn while making a heartfelt wish, the wish is said to come true. Wands of hazel wood will provide poetic inspiration.

Holly

Holly is the sacred tree associated with the Winter Solstice. It symbolizes peace, goodwill, and happiness. The custom of decorating one's house with holly at Yule first began with the Romans who packed their gifts for Saturnalia in holly leaves.

A love spell requires the seeker to go out at midnight, in absolute silence, and gather nine, smooth holly leaves (known as she-holly). The leaves must be folded in a three-cornered handkerchief and tied with nine knots. This packet is placed under the seeker's pillow and, as long as the seeker remains silent until dawn, he or she will dream of their future mate.

The Holly King, who represents dying vegetation, is defeated on the Winter Solstice by the Oak King. The Holly King, usually depicted as an old man, may be the precursor of Santa Claus.

Knowing and working with the nine sacred trees is a way to deepen our appreciation and further connect us with the green world.

The Norse Valkyries

......

BY D.J. CONWAY

Most people immediately identify the valkyries as Odin's Choosers of the Slain. In the beginning of the Norse religious tradition, the valkyries belonged to Freyja, and possibly Frigg, who were both spiritual beings and actual physical priestesses of the goddess. In the modern writings of those involved in Norse tradition, the valkyries have been relegated to the position of female servants to the god Odin. This was a much later designation of these warriors.

Today, we think of valkyries as otherworld beings who rode in the air over battlefields. Descriptions in the Norse poems and prose picture the valkyries as helmeted women with spears, crowned with flames and mounted on flying horses whose manes dropped dew or hail. They directed the course of battles and chose the valiant warriors for Valhalla. They could also turn themselves into swan-maidens. These warrior-women were often called death angels, swan-women, mare-women, and they were associated with horses, ravens, and wolves.

Some Norse writings say there were either nine (a moon number) or thirteen (a feminine mystical number) valkyries. However, several sources suggest that the number was limitless.

Sometimes the valkyries were called *oskmeyhar* (wish-women). Another word for these Norse warrior women was *sigewif*, or victory-women.

Like the *disir*, the valkyries should be classified as Freyja's priestesses. The disir and the valkyries were considered to be both spiritual entities and physical beings. As spirit guides, the disir appeared in dreams and were then referred to as spadisir. The Disablot (a festival held in their honor) was celebrated at the beginning of winter. Among the North Germanic tribes, the goddess Holda or Bertha, the same goddess as Hel, was considered to be the leader of the Wild Hunt. She was accompanied by her hounds and the valkyries.

German legends tell of warrior women who could bind or loose fetters (a type of curse), hold back the enemy, change the course of battle (fate), answer to spells to accomplish these tasks, ride through the air (astral travel?), and assume animal forms—all the same traits attributed to the valkyries. The valkyrie assuming animal form is not the same as the berserker. The berserkers were men who belonged to an Odin cult. Once these men took on the animal form, they exhibited little, if any, humanity. The shapeshifting valkyrie, however, never lost control. Sometimes she took her animal familiar's form in order to astral travel incognito. Other times she assumed the animal shape to carry messages to other psychics, pass on a warning or message to humans who might otherwise not heed her words, or gather information.

The valkyries were said often to appear in dreams or visions as a warning. It was they who helped work out the fate of humans, like the disir and the Norns.

Remaining records speak of the valkyries as both human and supernatural, thus pointing to the distinct possibility that there were physical warrior-priestesses called valkyries who represented their supernatural counterparts.

Those women who have a natural fierceness of spirit and determination, or those who develop such a spirit, will find in the valkyrie way a new opening for magical and spiritual growth. The ancient Norse peoples gave equal rights to both men and women. Outspoken women, some of whom fought beside the men in battle, were common. Using the power of the valkyries to take charge of your life, stand up for yourself, and develop a more rounded, power-charge personality is a positive step for any woman.

THE SUBTLE ART OF
MAGIC IN THE WORKPLACE

••••••

BY MICKIE MUELLER

It's Monday morning and you grab a cup of coffee as you hit the time clock. A million mundane thoughts begin to swarm into your mind about deadlines, company cutbacks, or that big inspection you have to get ready for. It all makes you wonder, as you clock in for work—do you really have to clock out the witch? As magical practitioners, we walk between the worlds, therefore that answer would be a resounding "no!"

Remove Negativity
Without Creating a Stir

Negative energy has a way of lurking around the workplace due to difficult customers and coworkers alike. Since negativity tends to build upon itself, it is wise to neutralize it before it gets out of hand. If you try the following little trick, pay extra attention throughout the day and see if the place feels nicer and tempers cool.

Purchase an ammonia-free glass cleaner with a vinegar base and pour out just a bit. If you can't find a vinegar-based product, just add a little white vinegar to regular glass cleaner. At home, place the following herbs in a hot cup of water: basil, lavender, sage, and just a pinch of sea salt. Feel free to substitute your favorite cleansing and protection herbs. Allow the mixture to steep for at least five minutes, strain through a coffee filter, and pour a small amount into the glass cleaner. (*Really strain it well:* any little chunks of herbs will clog up your sprayer.) Holding the bottle in both hands, raise energy by repeating the following chant and sending it into the bottle:

> *Herbs and vinegar do your best*
> *A cleansing mixture I request.*
> *Destroying negative energy*
> *As I spray and as I clean.*

When you arrive at work the next day, clean your work area with your enchanted cleaner as you repeat the chant in your head to reaffirm your purpose. Your boss will think you are quite industrious. Keep your magical spray at work and use it anytime, or when you feel the place is bogged down with negativity.

If negativity has already gotten the better of you, here are a couple ideas to magically blow off some steam. If you work in an office, it's time to shred some documents. As you hold the papers in your hands, shove all your angry, hurt, or frustrated feelings into the documents. As you drop them one by one into the paper shredder, feel all that psychic sludge destroyed with the sheets of paper. If you work in an environment with a box crusher, volunteer to take the boxes back to crush. As you place each box in the crusher, lightly blow your anger or bad feelings into the boxes. Visualize them as clear glass bubbles. Then hit the button and let the big machine crush those bad feeling to oblivion. Do you work in a restaurant? Easy! Just throw all your daily angst into a dish of leftover food and toss it right down the garbage disposal, followed by a slice of lemon and some salt. There are probably other ways you can come up with at your place of business to create the same result.

Computers, Machines, and Gadgets: We Love 'Em, We Hate 'Em

Most of us have to deal with some kind of machinery at work, be it a cash register, computer, pricing gun, or possessed coffee maker. When these workplace gadgets are functioning, they make our lives easier—but when they get fussy, they can make our workday very difficult. I currently work with a lot of problematic machinery, and I like to jokingly blame it on gremlins.

Sometimes equipment just seems to go haywire for no apparent reason, and while magic won't keep you from having to regularly care for equipment and call in the technician sometimes, you can keep problems to a minimum by sending positive energy into the machinery you work with. When we think about equipment, it is important to remember that everything is filled with energy, and that goes for both living and inanimate objects. Therefore, what you need to do to keep your mechanical devices going is basically noncellular healing.

Depending on your work environment, you may be able to bring a pretty crystal to work to set near your computer. If you can, it works great. Quartz crystals boost energy and raise positive vibrations. You can clean the crystal first at home by holding it under running water and visualizing all the negativity being washed away. My favorite method is to leave it outside in a rainstorm. Then you can magically charge it to boost your computer. Here is a simple chant you can use to charge your crystal, and you can also use it to boost the crystal at work if something seems to be going awry:

Shining stone, bright and clear,
Support machinery that lies near.
Protect and heal each circuit too,
And keep them running smooth and true.

If you're not in a situation where you can place a crystal near your workspace, try a penny. Copper is a magical metal that helps boost energy flow. But don't just grab one out of your pocket—it needs to be prepared first. A penny has gone through many hands and will need serious cleansing. Run it under cold water in the same manner as for a crystal, then bury it in some earth or a dish of salt for one month. If you choose to bury it in dirt, place a marker over it so you don't forget where you left it.

Now you can magically charge your penny. Anoint the penny with sandalwood or olive oil, and place it under a white candle. A tea light works great. You can use this chant:

Bright copper, metal of the earth,
Boost my machinery for all it's worth.
Good metal by all the elements cast,
Keep it all running and make it last.

Then place the penny in an inconspicuous place near or even under the computer or other equipment.

Another subtle method is the use of a magical symbol or rune. Good choices for symbols for healing your office equipment would be an equal armed cross, the "ansur" rune for communication, the "eolh" rune for protection, an infinity symbol, or any healing symbol you like. You can draw the symbol or symbols of your choice on the sticky side of a piece of opaque tape or sticker and then stick it to the problematic piece of equipment in a place you can easily reach, but that won't be obvious. Silently use this chant:

Magic symbols, powers stick,
Brightest blessings do the trick.

Place your hand over the tape to add to the charge any time you feel the need.

Personnel Communications

Sometimes interactions with those at work can become difficult due to stress, or even personality clashes. You may experience difficult coworkers, clients, or customers, but before you try to set that pricing gun to "stun" let's discuss some ways to keep personal relationships at work from getting out of hand.

First let's start with something that nearly everyone has experienced. Have you ever had a day at work when it seems like everyone is acting erratic, crabby, or just plain weird? Then suddenly a coworker says, "What's up with everyone today, is there a full moon or something?" Little do they know that you are all too aware of the moon's phase, and sometimes on those days it is indeed full.

You won't usually notice that it is the kind of day where everyone is a little "off" until you have gotten well into the day. The minute that you realize, "Man, everyone is so crabby today," it is time to act. Make any excuse to head for the front door, and as you walk toward it, chant the word "balance" in your head over and over. The walking will raise energy, so feel it build in the center of your chest. When you reach the door, touch it and release the energy as you repeat "balance" once more in your head, followed by "So mote it be." Most people who walk through that door will feel that balancing energy and be less likely to fall under the influence of whatever is causing personality anomalies. You can also do a similar kind of spell by raising the "balance" energy and sending it as you do a page over the loudspeakers. Most people within the sound of your voice will feel a soothing effect, and things should calm down a bit.

You will notice that I said "most people." That is because this is not manipulative magic. Most people really don't want to be crabby and unbalanced, so they will benefit from their own wish to take the opportunity to find balance. There are a few people who are so attached to their anger that they are not willing to give it up. That is their choice, but to try to force the issues would be manipulative and unethical. When dealing with others it is very important to remember to act ethically.

Perhaps you have been in a situation at work where you feel that your voice is not being heard. You have a great idea, or want to discuss a raise or promotion, but you feel that your words just aren't getting through. Before you go to work that day, spend a few minutes on this simple meditation. Lie down on your back and place a blue stone of your choice at the base of your throat. Close your eyes and visualize a beam of bright, warm light coming down from the sky and shining down into your throat chakra. Your throat chakra is the energy vortex that enhances communication and expression. Feel it filling with energy, becoming stronger. When you feel the energy in your throat chakra is glowing and strong, you are done. Carry the stone in your pocket when you go to work, and let the communication begin.

Don't Take It Home with You

Okay, you had a rough day at work, despite your efforts to keep things running smoothly—hey, it happens. You have a lot on your mind and all you want to do is go home and relax. But everything you had to deal with is still on your mind. There is no reason to take it home with you—what's done is done.

So find a place to pull the car over safely for about five minutes (a well-lit gas station works fine). Lock the doors and relax. Visualize a red balloon on a string before you. As you inhale slowly through your nose, exhale through your mouth and "blow" all that anxiety into the balloon. See it getting larger and larger as you fill it with everything that bothered you that day. When everything you wish to rid yourself of has gone into the balloon, imagine a lovely pair of scissors in your hand, decorative and magical. Reach out with your hand and cut the string with the scissors as you say "snip" and see it float away. It passes through the atmosphere and into space as the gravity of the sun catches it and pulls it in. All your anxiety is incinerated in the blazing sun and will be turned into neutral energy. Now take a deep breath, go home, relax, and recharge. Tomorrow is another day.

When you get to work the next day, take your inner witch with you. When you form a true relationship with your magical self, you can take that part of yourself everywhere. Remember that the kind of magic that is most effective at work is subtle. Intention is very important, and this kind of magic helps to train your mind to work without all the bells and whistles. The magic is always in you.

INTRODUCTION TO GEOMANCY

......

BY JOHN MICHAEL GREER

Geomancy is the forgotten oracle of the Western world. Few people know about it nowadays, but geomancy was among the most common methods of divination through the Middle Ages and Renaissance. It was imported to Europe from the Muslim world with the first wave of translations from Arabic in the early twelfth century, and spread quickly. Hundreds of geomantic manuals survive in manuscript collection, and these are only a small fraction of the total number that were once in circulation.

Like the Chinese *I Ching*, and other less widely known methods of divination, geomancy is based on binary processes—that is, processes that can give rise to one of two different answers. The "divination system" of flipping a coin is a very simple example of this. More complete methods combine some set number of binary events (even and odd numbers, for example) to produce a pattern that communicates meaning to the diviner.

In geomancy, four binary events were added together to produce patterns of meaning. There were sixteen of these patterns, or figures, and they made up the basic building blocks of geomancy. These, with their traditional meanings, are as follows:

The Geomantic Figures

Name	Figure	Qualities
Puer (boy)	• • • • •	Rashness, violence, energy, destructiveness. Generally unfavorable except in matters of love and war.
Amissio (loss)	• • • • • •	Transience and loss. Favorable for love and for situations in which loss is desired, but unfavorable for material matters.
Albus (white)	• • • • • • •	Peace, wisdom, purity; a favorable figure, but weak. Good for beginnings and business ventures.
Populus (people)	• • • • • • • •	Multitude, a gathering or assembly of people. Good with good, evil with evil; a natural figure neither favorable nor unfavorable.

Name	Figure	Qualities
Fortuna Major (greater fortune)	• • • • • •	Great good fortune, inner strength. A figure of power and success, favorable for any form of competition.
Conjuncio (conjunction)	• • • • • •	Combination of forces or people; recovery of lost things. A neutral figure, neither favorable nor unfavorable.
Puella (girl)	• • • • •	Harmony and happiness; a favorable figure in nearly all questions.
Rubeus (red)	• • • • • • •	Passion, power, fierceness, and vice. Evil in all that is good and good in all that is evil.
Acquisitio (gain)	• • • • • •	Success, profit, and gain; things within one's grasp. Favorable in nearly all matters.
Carcer (prison)	• • • • • •	Restriction, delay, limitation, imprisonment. An unfavorable figure.
Tristia (sorrow)	• • • • • • •	Sorrow, suffering, illness, and pain. An unfavorable figure except in questions relating to building and the earth.

Name	Figure	Qualities
Laetitia (joy)	• • • • • • •	Happiness and health. A favorable figure.
Cauda Draconis (tail of the dragon)	• • • • •	A doorway leading out. Favorable for losses and endings, but an unfavorable figure in most questions. Brings good with evil, evil with good.
Caput Draconis (head of the dragon)	• • • • •	A doorway leading in. Favorable for beginnings and gain, neutral in other questions. Good with good, evil with evil.
Fortuna Minor (lesser fortune)	• • • • • •	Outward strength, help from others. Good for any matter a person wishes to proceed quickly.
Via (way)	• • • •	Change, movement, alteration of fortune. Favorite for journeys and voyages.

In geomantic practice, these figures are produced by what amounts to a simple form of automatic writing. Traditionally, the geomancer would smooth out an area of sand or bare soft ground and take a pointed stick in one hand, then concentrate on the question the divination was intended to answer. The diviner would then seek a sort of mental clarity in which no thought would rise up to disturb the process. Holding this state, he or she would make the stick move so that it made a line of marks across the ground. It is important that the geomancer not count the marks while they are being made.

Once four lines of marks are traced on the ground, the diviner then counts up the number of marks in each line. An odd number of marks equal a single point; an even number, a double point. The result might look something like this:

Line	Marks	Figure
First line	12 marks	• •
Second line	14 marks	• •
Third line	9 marks	•
Fourth line	13 marks	•

The result, in this case, is the geomantic figure Fortuna Major, the greater fortune.

The same thing can be done using paper and a pen. Several other processes have also been put to use—for example, some geomancers take a random handful of pebbles from a small bag or bowl, and then count the pebbles to see whether they came to an even number or an odd one. Decks of geomantic cards have also been used at various times. There were even special dice made with either one or two points on each face; four of them would be rolled to make a figure.

There are various ways to use these figure in a reading. The standard methods involved generating four of them—thus, making sixteen lines of points to start with—and then combining them in various ways to generate a total of sixteen figures, each of which makes it own contributions to the final reading. Done this way, a geomantic divination can be as detailed and informative as any form of divination in the world.

There's also a place, though, for a simpler approach. It can be useful simply to concentrate on a question, clear your mind, make four lines of dots, and interpret the future that results as an answer to the question. Thought this does have its limitations—in particular, the questions asked this way should be answerable with a "yes" or a "no"—it also provides a good introduction to the secret of the "forgotten oracle."

LABYRINTH

......

BY EMELY FLAK

Imagine taking a walk to the core, where you journey on foot paths that take you forward and back in a circular pattern. Finally, you reach the center, but this is not the end of your journey. Instead, it's only just beginning as you reflect, contemplate, meditate, pray, or simply relax. When you are ready, you walk again, retracing in reverse, the same steps that brought you to the center to return to your starting point. You have taken the walk that represents birth, death, and rebirth. You have walked the sacred labyrinth. Carl Jung once referred to the labyrinth symbol as an archetype of transformation.

Throughout history, across various locations around the globe, the labyrinth pattern has been found on cave walls, coins, pottery, cathedral floors, fabric and basket weaves, and in outdoor structures, suggesting that this sacred design has been a potent symbol in many cultures. The labyrinth is recognized as a magical geometric form, on par with structures such as the ancient pyramids and Stonehenge. Because they have been constructed by many cultures over thousands of years, some claim the labyrinth represents a universal pattern in human consciousness.

Characteristics

The labyrinth pattern is usually in the form of a circle, with circular, meandering pathways to its core. A labyrinth is typically described as unicursal, meaning one path. The pathway that takes you to the core is the same one that returns you back out. As the labyrinth is often confused with a maze, it's important to make the distinction. A maze is designed to confuse. With its twists and dead ends, the maze is a puzzle that tests memory and persistence, making it a left-brain task demanding analysis and logical thought. Contrast this with the labyrinth that features only one path and no trickery. Whilst a maze can stimulate and confuse you, the labyrinth soothes and balances without the distraction or stress associated with decision-making. When walking the labyrinth, you make turns of 180 degrees, which not only shift your direction, but also shift your awareness from left to right brain. Through these mind shifts engaging both sides of the brain, you are transported to a state of relaxed alertness, making you more receptive to a meditative state. It is also believed that this open state of consciousness helps balance the chakras.

Although each labyrinth is designed differently, most feature one of the two main patterns. The main ones are the seven-circuit classical labyrinth (the ancient form) and the more recent eleven-circuit design that appeared during medieval times. Interestingly, in some literature, the seven-circuit form has been linked with the seven chakras of the body. The circuit describes the path or ring that leads to the center. In history, the more famous ones appear in mythology in the story of King Minos at the Palace of Knossos in Crete, along with actual representations of the labyrinth pattern that are believed to exist in buildings in ancient Egypt. In the Middle Ages, the labyrinth enjoyed a revival, appearing in Gothic cathedrals in the more complex pattern of eleven circuits.

Symbolism

As the spiral circle in the labyrinth pattern is an ancient symbol for the divine mother, the symbol is believed to represent the sacred feminine. The labyrinth walk can represent both Mother Earth and Triple Goddess. As you walk to the core, you symbolically enter another world. As you return, you are reborn to experience the end of one state and the beginning of another, making it a symbol for life, death, and rebirth. In the Hopi Indian culture, the labyrinth symbolized Mother Earth and the underground world out of which their people emerged. The knowledge to walk the labyrinth, to its core and back, was regarded as an ability to travel to the other world. In this cultural context, the center was believed to be the mother's belly—a place of birth.

As a design that is typically circular and combined with spiral patterns, the labyrinth expresses a visual image of wholeness and natural cycles. Interestingly, the labyrinth pattern has been likened in design to the Buddhist mandalas. In Buddhism, a mandala, circular in design with a focus on its center, is a visual meditation aid as it depicts a physical representation of the spiritual realm.

History

In Roman history, mosaics portrayed labyrinths as fortified cities, making the pattern a symbol of protection appearing above doorways. In this culture, the design was often adapted in a square shape, also appearing as patterns on floors. In mythology, the labyrinth features in the story of King Minos of Crete. The labyrinth design, created as a structure with walls, was built to hold the Minotaur—a fearful creature that was half man and half bull. Eventually, the hero, Theseus, takes the brave journey into the labyrinth to kill the monster. The Minotaur at the center of the labyrinth appears on ancient coins and gems dating from this period. In this context, the successful return journey to the core represents courage and victory.

Religion

In Gothic cathedrals during medieval times, the labyrinth emerged as the more intricate eleven-circuit design divided into four quadrants. The most famous of these, built around 1200, can be visited today at Chartres Cathedral, near Paris. It is believed that this floor labyrinth, in a Christian setting, was walked to represent a quest to connect with the divine, and to replace an actual pilgrimage to Jerusalem as it was named *Chemin de Jerusalem*, which means "Road to Jerusalem." By taking this simulated pilgrimage, you would be transformed, leaving the old you behind and emerging ready for new beginnings in your life's journey. As additional penance, some pilgrims walked the labyrinth on their knees. This exercise would take about an hour, or the time needed to walk three miles.

During the same medieval period, about 500 labyrinths as stone structures, emerged in Scandinavia, most found near the coast. As secular constructions, they were believed to be built by fishing communities to trap evil-spirited trolls and winds in the spirals, for protection of the fishermen at sea. In recent times, the labyrinth has appeared in contemporary churches, such as Grace Cathedral in San Francisco and in the King Lutheran Church in Torrance, California. Today, you will come across labyrinths in gardens, parks, and meditation retreats and in respite facilities or hospitals as a healing tool.

The Labyrinth Walk

Each time you take a walk through a labyrinth you will experience it differently. You can take as long as you wish. Some journeys will be shorter than others depending on your purpose, intent, and response to your journey. If you can, take the journey barefoot to connect with the earth's energies as you walk. Quintessentially, the walk represents a form of pilgrimage to the symbolic center for recovery or enlightenment. The return passage back to the entrance symbolizes rebirth, recovery, or liberation.

Each time you walk the labyrinth it may be for a different reason. You may be seeking:

- Balancing or centering
- Healing
- Connection to higher self
- Contemplation
- Focus
- Meditation
- Prayer
- Help with a decision
- Opening awareness

Once you reach the center of the labyrinth, or at the conclusion of your journey, you can experience:

- Relaxation

- Answers, solutions, or insight

- Sense of peace and present being

- Warmth

- Liberation

- Energy

- Empowerment

- Healing or recovery

If you cannot find a labyrinth near you to walk, you can simulate a walk on various websites or trace one with your finger. Alternatively, get together with some friends and draw one in the sand or create one on the ground with twigs, sticks, or chalk markings. Take the journey and see where it takes you!

The labyrinth is both secular and spiritual. With no alignment with a specific religious path, the symbol is a powerful one across all cultures and beliefs. As an exercise, the labyrinth walk provides numerous experiences that meet varied needs. Overall, the sacredness of the pattern and the walk helps us experience a greater sense of oneness and being, making it a metaphor for the movement of spirit in our life.

AIR

THE SACRED POWER
OF YOUR NAME

••••••

BY TED ANDREWS

Wouldn't it be wonderful if you could discover an ancient word or phrase that would solve all your life problems, instill wealth and prosperity, or bring love into your life? Our myths and tales are filled with individuals seeking that one word or phrase that would make life magickal and wondrous. There still abides in every man, woman, and child a deep-seated, ancient memory of the reality of the power of the *word*.

The essential power of sound and words is common to all forms of high and low magick. Word magick is universal, and whether we realize it or not, we were each given our own "magical word" at birth. This word can balance you physically and spiritually. It can awaken you to your highest potential. It reveals your primary lessons in life, and it pinpoints the easiest path to fulfill-ment. This magickal word is your name!

Ancient traditional and societies recognize that to "know" the name of something was to have knowledge and power over it, but this meant knowing all aspects of it. Name Magick is the process of understanding the significance of all the elements within your name and the archetypal energies to which they align you. It involves attaching definite meanings to the sounds, the scripts, and their combinations to invoke certain plays of energy within your life.

Your individual names contain much power, and if you come to know them properly, you can discover much about your own soul's purpose and how to release your spiritual energies more strongly within your individual physical life circumstances. The meanings, the sounds, the rhythms, the nature of the letter, and all of the combinations disclose secrets about an individual's es-sence—past and present, physical and spiritual.

The first name is your most powerful and individually creative energy. It reveals the identifying and creative essence of the soul. The family name, or surname, indicated lessons and energies in-herited from your ancestors and parents. The middle name is a re-flection of your other abilities and tasks that may have to be dealt with in your life. Together they indicate the motives, knowledge, and potential you have come to awaken and use to walk your life's path. Your name reflects an energy matrix that will be working and evolving within during this incarnation.

Affirming Your Essence

The meaning of your name is of great significance. It is symbolic of specific energies you can work to unfold to affirm your true essence. It is a practice that is both balancing and energizing. It is an excellent prelude to any form of meditation.

To use your own name in an "I am" phrase is strengthening, protective, and creative. It reestablishes the link between you in your physical life and the diving part of you that is a portion of all energies and light within the universe. The "I am" phrase draws its power from a Hebrew name for God—EHEIEH, which means "I am that I am." In the Hebrew Qabala it is a link to the most spiritual level of the subconscious mind. When you use it in an affirmation with your name, you are activating the most spiritual energies of your essence. For example, the name TRACY means "to reap; industrious."

"I am Tracy! I reap the rewards of life."

or

"I am Tracy!
I am the industrious child of the Divine!"

The Power of the Mystical Vowels

The vowels are the *activating life force* of the name. In most of the ancient alphabets the vowels were sacred, and often they were not included within the alphabet itself. The vowels indicated the soul potential we have come to unfold. The shape, the sound, the color, and the astrological correspondence all provide clues to the lessons and abilities you must meet and unfold in your own unique way.

The primary vowel in your name is your major force. This is the vowel sound most strongly within your first name. It is the keynote of your soul essence.

The Vowel A—Illumination

This is a vowel associated with the colors white or gold. It is linked to the element of ether and the energies of the sun. It is a symbol of diving unity. It reflected the intellectual, one who strives for truth, and is ambitious. It reflects versatility and many talents. Its energies can be scattering, and it can bring lessons in concentration, hypersensitivity, possessiveness, and lack of will. It also makes some idealist, inventive, creative, and broad-minded. It is tied to the energies of higher clairvoyance, control of the elements, and even levitation.

The Vowel E—Strength and Self-Mastery

The vowel *E* is associated with the color blue, the element of air and the planet Mercury. It reflects the energies of higher perception gained through chastity. It is the energy of the mystic, the poet, and the lover of truth. It gives wondrous strength on the higher planes. It brings lessons in narrow-mindedness, dogmatism, and deceit. It also makes one inherently intuitive, philosophical, and electrical in nature. It is tied to the archetypal energies that open true clairaudience and time perception, along with the understanding of the language of animals.

The Vowel I—Divine Love

The vowel *I* is associated with the color of red-violet, the element of fire, and the planet Mars. It gives physical, mental, and/or spiritual strength that can be used for strong healing. It makes for an original and unique mentality. It brings lessons in becoming without possessing. Those with this as the predominant vowel have a great capacity for attracting love. It can manifest lessons in possessiveness, impulsiveness, and distrust. It also makes one self-sufficient, stimulating, and catalytic in the lives of others. These individuals can learn to understand and control the law of cause and effect.

The Vowel O—Divine Justice and Balance

This vowel is associated with the color black, the element of water, and the planet Saturn. It brings lessons in the ideal vs. the real. It gives the individual the ability to bind together and connect. There is great sensitivity and imagination. These individuals should only focus on what they wished to be created, as they have a powerful ability to manifest that which they visualize. This vowel brings lessons in lack of will, fear of failure, and oversensitivity to criticism. It also makes one psychic and sympathetic, and it gives a strong sense of justice. The *O* is the womb in which new life is created.

The Vowel U—Birth-Giving

This vowel is associated with the element of earth, all Earth-tone colors, and the planets Earth and Venus. The *U* gives the energy to provide protection through resistance. It can resist any invasion; thus, those with this as a predominant vowel need love, patience, and gentleness to open to the new. Harshness will crush them. These individuals have strong intuitions and are excellent judges of character. Dream work is essential for these individuals as their dreams are highly significant. They can learn to control them.

The Vowel Y—Transmutation

This vowel is associated with the elements of fire and water, the planets Mars and Venus, and the color of light golden brown (wheat). The *Y* is only a vowel when sounded in a name. It holds the lesson of freedom from bondage and freedom through discipline. It is the letter for bringing the male and female into balance and union so that the holy child within can be born. These individuals must be gently guided as they are ruled by love. They have come to build newer and stronger mental powers. They often have a great capacity for manifesting power—positive or negative.

The sounds that the vowels make within your name can indicate even more aspects of your own essence. The vowel sounds also indicate which chakra centers you have come to work most with during this incarnation. These reflect physiological aspects as well as spiritual. (Refer to the chart on page 107.)

Your Name Rhythms

Your name has a rhythm that also resonates with more universal and natural rhythms of life. To determine your name's rhythm, write out your full name as it appears on your birth certificate, then divide it into syllables. Using the Table of Rhythmic Correspondences on the following page, determine what natural and universal rhythms you are not harmonious with in this incarnation.

Table of Rhythmic Correspondences

Rhythms	Energies, Effects, and Lessons
1	Aligns one to archetypal male energies; initiator; strength of will; discrimination; inventiveness; self-centeredness; laziness; fearfulness or fearlessness; lessons and energies of confidence; searching for answers; independence and originality.
2	Aligns one to rhythms of astral plane, archetypal feminine energy, and dream consciousness; cooperation; kindness; psychic sensitivity; hypersensitivity; can be scattering; a need to focus on details; vacillation and lessons of divisiveness; passion.
3	Aligns one to rhythms of saints and blessed souls; energies of art/inspiration; creativity; lessons of wastefulness and repression; spirituality and the awakening of the inner child; expressiveness (good or bad); optimism.
4	Aligns one to the rhythms of the devas and divine men; energies of harmony/balance; building with patience; restricting and insensitive; narrow-mindedness; impracticality; solidarity; integration of energies, learnings from four corners of Earth.
5	Aligns one to rhythms to Mother Nature; awakening of the universe; awakening of the microcosm of soul; lessons of freedom and purity; versatility; scattered; resists change and imposes rules; healing; adventuresome; freeing from limitations; psychic powers.
6	Aligns one with the feminine/mothering energies of the universe; nurturing energies; healing; birth-giving energy rhythms on all levels; rhythms of the educator; cynical and worrisome lessons; responsibility and reliability.

Rhythms	Energies, Effects, and Lessons
7	Aligns one to the energies of all people and all planes; rhythms of healing for all systems; lessons of self-awareness and truth; rhythms of strong intuition; lessons of criticalness, melancholy, and inferiority; wisdom and knowledge.
8	Aligns one to the energies of the gods and goddesses as they worked through nature in the past; unites physical rhythms of individual with spiritual ones; confidence; occult power; lessons of carelessness and authority; awakens true judgment of character.
9	Aligns one to all healing energies and experiences; rhythm of empathy and transitional forces in the universe; lessons of being hurt and overly sensitive; pessimism and indifference; intuitive love; rhythms of at-one-ment.

Table of Vowel Correspondences

Vowel Glyph	Vowel Sounds	Chakras	Effects of Energy When Activated
A	ay (hay)	Heart	Chest, lungs, circulation, heart, blood (Love, Healing, Balance, Akashic Memory)
	ah (cat)	Throat	Throat, respiration, mouth, trachea, etc. (Creative Expression, Clairaudience)
	aw (saw)	Solar Plexus	Stomach, digestion, left-brain, intestines (Inspiration, Clairsentience, Psychism)

Vowel Glyph	Vowel Sounds	Chakras	Effects of Energy When Activated
E	ee (see)	Brow	Head cavity, sinuses, brain, pituitary glands (Clairvoyance, Third Eye, Spiritual Vision)
		Crown	Skeletal system, pineal (Christ Consciousness)
	eh (set)	Throat	Throat, respiration, mouth, trachea, etc. (Creative Expression, Clairaudience)
I	I (eye)	Medulla Oblongata	Balanced brain function, mental clarity (Mind over Emotions, "Intelligence of Heart")
	ih (bit)	Throat	Throat, respiration, mouth, trachea, etc. (Creative Expression, Clairaudience)
O	oh (note)	Spleen	Muscular system, reproduction, navel area (Creativity, Reserve Energy, Higher Emotional)
	aw (cot)	Solar Plexus	Stomach, digestion, left-brain, intestines (Inspiration, Power, Psychic Sensitivity)
U	oo (boot)	Base	Genitals, pelvis, lower body, circulation (Vitality, Life Force, Kundalini)
	uh (but)	Throat	Throat, respiration, mouth, trachea, etc. (Creative Expression, Clairaudience)

Uncovering the mystery of your name and its effects within your life is a high form of esoteric initiation. Learning to use it to bridge the spiritual to the physical is the epitome of the spiritual path. It is said that when the student is ready the teacher will appear. Working with your own name rings the doorbell of your inner teacher. To hear the angels sing, you must first hear the song without your own heart. It is the song echoed within your name.

Powwow Healing Chants

······

by Silver RavenWolf

Chants are vital to the healing process. Most charms and spells in powwow require the chant to be said thrice. After each chant, the healer blows his or her breath three short times toward the client and often writes a sigil in the air over the body. Whether you are Buddhist, Christian, Jewish, or Wiccan, the chants will work if your faith is firm.

The All-Purpose Chant

If you don't know what is wrong with the person, this is the best chant to use. Recite the chant three times. At each stanza, you must blow your breath at the wound three times in quick succession. You may end the chant with "In the name of the Father, Son, and Holy Ghost" as Preston did, or you can end it with the connection to your own deity system. It will work either way.

Don't forget to seal the chant in the end with the equal-armed cross motion with your finger.

Begin by saying the full name of the patient.

Hest thou recovered health and goddess
I will lead thee again to the Maiden,
    Mother, and Crone.
Therefore so help thee our Goddess readily
And thou shalt be blessed as well as
    the chalice of ale and holy cakes
Which Aradia offered to her followers
    before she left them.
Therefore so help you
Maiden, Mother, and Crone.

Repeat most chants in three- to fifteen-minute intervals, depending upon the seriousness of the problem. For example, a powwow may heal thusly:

1. Repeat the client's full name.

2. Say the primary chant once.

3. Say the secondary chant once.

4. Repeat the primary chant.

5. Repeat the secondary chant.

6. Repeat the primary chant.

7. Repeat the secondary chant.

8. Give the appropriate signage to seal the healing.

9. Wait three to fifteen minutes.

10. Begin the procedure again and complete.

11. Wait three to fifteen minutes.

12. Begin the procedure again and complete.

The interval method is to allow the participants to recharge their magical batteries. Not all powwows use the three- to fifteen-minute break—some go straight through, taking up to twenty minutes to complete the hands-on healing.

I think there are as many chants for stopping blood as there are powwows. Although you might not believe it, it is an easy technique to learn and is often the first taught by a powwow.

Holy Mary Mother of God
Who stoppeth the pain and stoppeth the blood.
In the name of the Maiden, Mother, and Crone.
So be it.
Blessed wound
Blessed hour
Blessed be the day the goddess came to power.
Women's mysteries fine and strong
Stop this blood through female song.

Use the chant listed next in dire emergencies. It is good for all emergency medical situations.

Aradia walked before (give the person's name)
And she saw (the person's name)
Lying in blood and pain.
She spoke and said, "Thou shalt live,
    thou shalt live, thou shalt live."
And it was done.
In the name of the Maiden, Mother, and Crone.
And the father, son, and holy ghost.
So mote it be.

I think the most astounding chant is the one below. Many of us have used the chant for a variety of purposes, from bee stings to more serious medical conditions. I'd like to remind you to seek proper medical treatment in tandem with healing magic.

(Disease/injury) come of the marrow into the bones
Out of the bones into the blood
Out of the blood into the flesh
Out of the flesh upon the skin
From the skin and into (the person's name) hair
Out of the hair into the green forest
Out of the green forest into the dry sand
As sure as the god moves within the goddess
and out into the world.

When you are pulling sickness, pain, or disease out of another person, you should direct it out from your body and away from his or her body. No one should be in the "line of fire" as previously mentioned. If there are other people in the room, it really is best if they leave before you begin. The only exception is parents of children who will need support.

This chant leads the subconscious mind of the healer in small steps through the healing process. It enables you to take one movement of the disease at a time. It allows your subconscious to connect with step-by-step imagery.

Remember to seek adequate medical care immediately. However, it doesn't hurt to have the goddess on your side.

The Morrigan:
War Goddess of the Celts

......

by Christie M. Wright

In Celtic society, women played a very important role. Equal to men, they could own land, obtain a divorce and not be left penniless, and fight in battles. They were mothers, lovers, warriors, hunters, politicians, leaders, and much, much more.

It seems natural that their goddess of war should be feminine entity. I should say goddesses, for the Morrigan is a triple-figure composed of Macha, Badb, and Nemain. Collectively, their name means the "phantom queen," probably due to their uncanny powers of shapeshifting.

In looking at the three goddesses of the Morrigan, one can see the mother in Macha, whose name means "battle." While pregnant with twins, she was forced to run a race against the two fastest horses in Ireland, incidentally mares. She won the race, but died while giving birth afterward. With her last breath, she cursed the men of Ulster to have great labor pains whenever danger threatened.

Macha may also be equated to Brighid, another triple entity. Macha, like Brighid, possessed a sacred shrine in which an eternal flame was tended by temple maidens; both shrines were eventually taken over by nuns who kept the flame living, yet changed the name of the deity to whom the shrines were devoted.

Badb, on the other hand, is an extremely powerful goddess whose name means "one who boils," linking her to the otherworld cauldron over which she is said to preside. In Celtic belief, it is Badb who will bring about the end world destruction by causing the great cauldron to boil over, drowning the planet and all creatures upon it.

Badb belongs to two triplicities: the Fury and the Morrigan, playing the part of the hag in each. She is linked with the *Beansidhe* (English banshee), a faery of death who was often seen at a ford, washing the armor of those who would die in the battle ahead. It is said that on Samhain Badb can tell you the time of your death should you wish it.

Little is said of Nemain, save that her name means "venomous one," and that she is a crone goddess.

When battle ensued, the Morrigan would sometimes fly over the field in the form of a crow or raven, watching eagerly for carrion, and screeching to cause the slain to move about in a grotesque dance. Her harvest consisted of trophies of slain warriors.

There might even be a link between the Greek goddess of war, Athena, and the Celtic Morrigan. Each can be seen as a personification of the culture in which she existed. The Greeks were philosophical by nature, so it stands to reason that their goddess of war would not run into battle screeching and calling for blood. As it is, Athena is often depicted wearing a long white tunic with hardly any armor, and a snow white owl perched upon her shoulder. The Morrigan likely entered the battle naked, as did her warriors, screaming like a banshee and killing any enemy that dared to move. The Celts were a wild people, governed by the natural world with all its danger, while the Greeks appeared to live in a kingdom of clouds. Both goddesses were a product of their society and each served their purposes for the people.

It is best to work with the goddesses of the Morrigan one at a time as their collective energies are powerfully dangerous. One may call on them for passing over rituals, or to aid in overcoming an enemy. Servicemen and women may call on them when entering battle. Symbols of the Morrigan include the raven, crow, obsidian, and rubies, the waning and dark moons, nightshade, henbane, and black dogs.

The Morrigan has much to teach, and like any teacher, commands respect. Remember, the Morrigan is a potent force that must be treated with care and caution.

Alternative Sabbat
Celebrations

......

by Estelle Daniels

The eight sabbat celebrations all have their traditions. The Yule log is burned on the Winter Solstice to symbolize the warmth of nature in a cold and dead part of the year. Eggs are painted on Ostara to celebrate nature's rebirth.

That is to say, the sabbats are based upon an agrarian model, and nature worship is inherent in the dance of the seasons. But the modern world is ironically, for the most part, an indoor world.

This is the impetus for creating a series of alternative sabbat celebrations that have to do with being outdoors and working with the seasons. The following suggestions are based upon a four-season year. Some localities have years with just three, or even two seasons, and growing and planting occurs at different times. Adapt your outdoor sabbat celebrations to the individual climate of your locality.

Samhain

Samhain is the season of the root harvest, and also of the hunting season. For this sabbat, consider taking up hunting—you can use a camera if you'd rather not carry an actual gun. Just getting out into the woods in the fall and observing how nature is getting ready to bed down for the winter can give you a good Samhain feeling. Once you are outdoors, watch the sights and listen to the sounds. This is the time that birds migrate. Make a point of learning which birds go and which stay. Afterwards, make up a thick stew with veggies (and meat, if you eat it). This is a good and warming way to celebrate winter root crops.

Yule

Yule is the dark time of the year. Sitting vigil on the longest night with a Yule fire is one way to celebrate this sabbat. Fire is a sacred thing, and necessary for life. But modern society has tamed fire, so it's no longer the big deal it once was. A good alternative Yule celebration involves getting up before dawn after the longest night of the year, and gathering at a place with a good eastern view to green the sun as it comes up. Some ancient societies felt that this sun greeting was crucial to ensure its constant return. Alternatively, go ice skating, skiing, or sledding outdoors on this day and enjoy what the season has to offer. Then come in and drink warm cider, celebrating the fruits of an earlier season and appreciating the comforts of central heating.

Imbolc

Imbolc is the traditional time for working on the tools necessary for the coming year. Clean out your chests and closets, and sift through your Book of Shadows and other tools. Review and reorganize your magical stuff. Imbolc is also usually the coldest time of the year in northern climes. Go outside and watch the stillness of the world now. If the sun is out, it will be strong enough to melt ice and snow even if the temperature is below freezing. How does the old snow look compared to when it was new? If you get one of those rare warm days, a winter thaw, go outside and enjoy the sun and warmth. Feel the sun growing stronger, the days longer, and realize that spring and summer aren't far behind. Cook a meal using dried ingredients. In the past, this is the time people ate from their stores and reserves.

Ostara

Ostara is the Spring Equinox. If you can feel the spring's arrival, go outside and see how things are changing. Are the buds swelling on the trees? Are there flowers poking out of the snow? Watch the animals, are they more active after the winter. Are they mating? Building nests? Are fish running in your area? Watch the birds migrating back from the south, closing the cycle of the year.

Beltane

Beltane is when spring has arrived. The plants and trees are now in flower, so it's a perfect time to go out. Look at the new plants and at how the old plants are putting on new growth. Check what survived and what did not over the winter. Have a picnic outside if it's warm enough. Go to a farmers' market and get some first fruit: asparagus, strawberries—whatever grows first in your area. Eating foods in season in your locality is one way to keep your body in tune with nature. Make yourself a spring salad or tonic. Has fishing season started? Try going fishing. You can cook up what you catch, or just catch and release.

Midsummer

Midsummer is when the crops are in and fruit is more abundant. The first hay is usually ready. An outdoor picnic and walk is always fun. A trip to the swimming hole is fun too. On the longest day of the year, put a stick in the ground and see how short the shadow is at noon. Examine the sun. It is most closely overhead at noon on Midsummer in the Northern Hemisphere. You can stay up for the shortest night, having a party or just enjoying the warm weather. Go berry picking at a pick-your-own place. Eat some as you pick, and try to store some for the coming winter.

Lammas

Lammas is the first harvest and the height of summer. Crops are becoming ripe at the hottest time of the year. Camping is always fun now. Swimming cools your body naturally. This is the time for picnics and game. Ancient peoples celebrated these times with games and contests, which tested the people in preparation for coming hard months.

Mabon

Mabon is the main harvest. Go apple picking. Visit the farmers' market and see the bounty available in your area. Make a meal with only fresh foods harvested in your area. Give thanks for the bounty that is all around. Go outside and see how life is adapting and storing up resources for the winter to come. This is the main canning and preserving season. Try putting up something from your local food market.

SACRED RITUALS,
PUBLIC SPACES

......

BY DALLAS JENNIFER COBB

So much of our lives are lived in the public sphere, and while
many Pagan rituals and gatherings take place in private spaces,
there are times when a public space is the most fitting place for
a sacred ritual.

While living in Toronto's downtown west end, I took part in
many sabbat gatherings held in Dufferin Grove Park. As the name
implies, the space was a public park and natural spot that lent itself to festive gatherings. With tall stands of maple and oak trees, a
community garden area, adventure playground, and community
bake oven, the energy of the park was magical.

We found the space one autumn at equinox. My circle mates,
a relaxed and eclectic bunch, were eager to have a large fire as part

of the ritual and our gathering. Because most of us were apartment dwellers who lacked direct access to an outdoor space, Dufferin Grove was an ideal setting: lush, green, and accessible.

We went through the proper channels to get permission to use Dufferin Grove's fire pit. We went to the park authorities, applied for a fire permit, reserved the fire pit for the times and date we required, and described our gathering as a "festive celebration" on our application. Our request was approved and a permit issued—free of charge! We had only to identify two responsible people from our group who pledged to ensure that the fire was maintained safely and fully extinguished when we were finished. The park authorities even supplied the precut firewood for us, and stacked it neatly beside the fire pit.

After our initial sabbat in Dufferin Grove, the consensus was that we wanted to hold most of our sabbats and celebrations there—around the fire, under the oaks, in the open air, beneath the moon. Winter and summer, spring and fall, we found our way there in all seasons. Not just the open fire, but also the wide expanse of space, tall trees, and the feeling of empowerment that came from holding a sacred ritual in a public space thrilled us.

These days I live in a waterfront village of 1,700 people. A small rural community, there are few Pagans here. But that hasn't stopped my practice of magic ritual or public witchery. I have organized a baby-blessing ceremony on the public beach and done sabbat rituals in both the local provincial park and public beach. While my Pagan community here is much smaller, I have modified rituals to include more of my community, friends, and neighbors, but still utilizing public spaces in an effort to be both visible and magical. While my circle has shrunk, my sacred practice hasn't.

If you are thinking of coming out of the broom closet into the public realm, there are many things to consider when planning sacred rituals in public spaces. Part of the magic that we weave is the preparation and planning. We ready ourselves, the space, and our community for the upcoming ritual. But whatever the occasion, and whatever the setting, planning for safety and security are primary requirements for ensuring the sacred.

Finding a Magical Space

The best spot to practice magic is one that feels good to you and the people involved. Choose a physical space that holds good memories, meaning, or generally is associated with good happenings. A place that brings as many of the elements together in one spot is an idea ritual or celebration space. Whether you live in a city or a small rural village, these spots are there. You just need to look, and let your witchy senses be engaged.

Search for elements that lend themselves to your magic. Groves of trees honor the historic practice of magic that often took place within the security of groves. Water elements like streams and ponds are great, but even a fountain or a bucket of water to put out the fire can represent the element. Because our gatherings usually involved some dancing, my circle likes to have an open space large enough to accommodate us.

And don't forget the effect of ambient light. If you are gathering at night and want to see the moon, stars, and sky, choose a spot with natural darkness to make viewing the night sky possible.

Finally, think about practical stuff like where can people sit, and what there is to sit on. Grass is nice, but those with physical limitations like to have something up off the ground. The wonderful thing about parks is that there are often benches provided, or at least large logs like those around our fire pit.

Consecrating Public Space

Once you have found a suitable public space, how do you make it a sacred space? Parks and public lands are areas open to everyone and may be affected by divergent energies. It is important to work with the energy of the space before holding a ritual. Take the steps to sanctify the public place.

Like sanctifying yourself, it is important to purify and protect public spaces. Take the time to visit with space prior to the ritual. Walk the earth, intone your intention, and spread your energy throughout the space. Ask permission of the earth to celebrate there. Ask the gods and goddesses to join you, and ask for the protection of the fates.

Burn sage and sweet grass to clear old, stale energy, or sprinkle water to bless and consecrate the space. Once, when our usual fire pit had been in use up until our time to use it, members of my circle used branches from the community garden compost pile to symbolically sweep away the energy of the previous people and happenings.

It is also important to clear any dangerous objects from the space, so make sure you pick up any broken glass, sharp objects, or metal that could easily injure someone. And remove any garbage or trash that could draw down the energy.

Sacred Safety and Security

While most public spaces are safe, planning for safety and security is important for the people involved and for the energy of the ritual. Use your common sense. Make plans to arrive in twos or clusters, and depart in the same fashion. Provide clear directions so people don't get lost and end up wandering through some other area of the space. Dress in comfortable, functional clothing in case you need to gather more firewood, stomp out stray embers, or purposefully leave the presence of negative people.

Our circle always had a keeper of protection. That was the person designated to carry a small first-aid kit, a whistle, and a cell phone. These items are only needed in times of emergency and were rarely used, but provided us with a sense of safety and preparation. Our keeper was part of the ritual, but also had the role of keeping watch over any intruding energy and, where possible, diverting it from the group and the ritual.

Positive Pagan Images

There are a lot of negative images of magic and Pagans out there. I take it upon myself to try to balance out the misinformation not by fighting against the negative images, but by spreading my own positive images. The strongest magic is the transformation of thought or misconception, at will.

When planning a sabbat or a ritual, I try to imagine what it would look like from the outside to someone unfamiliar with the ritual. I want it to look inviting and interesting, so passersby feel intrigued and inquisitive, not frightened and angry. To give a gathering a lively, festive presence, I incorporate songs, chants, storytelling, and miming into a sabbat ritual.

When a gathering looks interesting, you may find people attracted to your circle and interested in joining you. If you are holding rituals in public spaces your circle will need to discuss, in advance, whether or not the ritual is open to visitors, and if so, during what parts of the ritual or celebration. Having clear agreement beforehand ensures that decisions are made for the good of the group and no one feels excluded.

During our sabbats in Toronto, we often had people wandering through the park join us. Attracted to the fire, the brightly garbed people, or perhaps intrigued by the chanting, singing, and storytelling, they drew near to watch. We had all agreed to open our circle at any time to include a wanderer. And this practice paid off. Several people became regularly involved with the circle and attended other sabbat celebrations.

So even if you live in close quarters and lack access to nature, it is possible to find a gorgeous natural setting for your rituals and gatherings. Spread the magic of the craft, and make plans to hold sacred rituals in public spaces, weaving safety and security into the fabric of the sacred.

RHYMES OF GOOD FORTUNE

......

by Laurel Nightspring Reufner

Find a penny, pick it up.
The rest of the day you'll have good luck.

What is our obsession with the finding of lucky objects? We did it as kids—and gleefully. My daughters are currently taken with pine cones, which are excitedly gathered and handed over to Mommy, sap and all. And perhaps the only thing that keeps us from obsession as adults is that we probably feel a little silly about it.

Lucky Stone Folklore

Perhaps this desire for lucky objects is genetic. Consider that it is only the rare small child who doesn't go through the rock collection phase. It doesn't matter what kind of stone or rock it is—driveway slag, river rocks, pea gravel. They all delight. Fortunately, as they get older children become more discerning and only certain kinds of stones will do for good luck. Eventually they have to be holey, white, round, or otherwise extraordinary.

Truth be told, my husband still scours the school playground for gravel for small stones with holes in them, although I seriously doubt he'd admit to gathering them for good luck. Most people keep their holey stones, but in some areas they are only lucky if you get rid of them. First you pick the stone up, then spit on it, and then throw it behind you while saying the following:

> *Lucky stone! Lucky stone! Go over my head,*
> *And bring me some good luck before I go to bed.*

Straight Pin Folklore

Finding a straight pin nowadays isn't all that big of a deal, unless it is stuck in the carpet where you were about to put your foot. But in fact, such pins were once prized treasures. They were difficult and expensive to make and buy, and so a woman's "pin money" was important. Therefore, finding a pin would indeed have been good luck. To leave one lying on the ground would be akin to walking past money. Consider also the solemn oath sworn on pain of "sticking a needle in your eye." Here are two rhymes about straight pins.

> *See a pin and pick it up*
> *All the day you'll have good luck.*
> *See a pin and let it lay*
> *Bad luck you'll have all that day.*
> *Pin, pin, bring me luck*
> *Because I stop to pick you up.*

Find a pin and let it lie,
You shall want before you die.
See a pin and let it lie,
Before the night you will cry.

If you find a pin, you are supposed to put it in your collar or lapel and wear it as long as you can. Alternatively, you can perform some pin-wishing magic. Making sure the pin is pointing toward you, pick it up with your right hand and stick it into the left shoulder of your clothing while making a wish. After you've worn the pin for a while, give it away to someone else or the wish won't come true. And be forewarned, some people believe that a pin should never be approached or picked up by its point, but only by the head.

Other Lucky Things

Find a feather, stick it up,
All the day you'll have good luck.

Buttons, coins, and four-leaf clovers are all also considered lucky to find. So are feathers considered lucky, especially the ones, as the above rhyme states, found stuck upright in the ground. Eagle feathers are especially lucky, but be sure to leave them where you find them, unless you have a permit to possess them.

And since they aren't all that prevalent today, finding a horseshoe is probably luckier now than it used to be. Some sources claim that you have to pitch the horseshoe over your head and make a wish, although I only see that leading to bad luck depending on where the horseshoe lands. And most of us probably already know that if you want to put a horseshoe up for good luck somewhere on your property, you need to nail it down with the points up so the luck doesn't run out.

Some lucky things, such as the first star in the night sky, cannot be picked up. Remember searching for it as a child and getting so excited when you beat your friends to it? Children today, as well as the young at heart everywhere, still enjoy this particular search.

Star light, star bright,
First star I see tonight,
Wish I may, wish I might,
Get this wish I wish tonight.

As many of us know, it is our intent that makes something lucky or unlucky. Children seem to have an uncanny knack for this, finding something during the course of the day that is unusual and makes them feel special. To find an unusual thing gives an extra little boost of confidence that today will be a good day. This is, of course, some of the greatest magic of all, for when we feel more confident our luck does seem better.

What about the penny that we started with? I still pick them up, most of the time. But only if they are lying face-up.

The Key to Your Dreams

......

by Janina Renée

Library shelves are overflowing with books that recount the fantastic adventures, wonderful insights, creative solutions, and poignant prophecies that other people have culled from their dreams. But suppose your own dreams are very prosaic—always the same old people, places, and situations. They don't seem to tell you anything that you don't already know. Here is an idea that may help open a new dimension to your dream world.

Keep an old skeleton or clack key by your bedside. Hang it perhaps from your bedpost by a purple ribbon, or keep it in some way close by so you can handle it and contemplate it a few moments before falling asleep.

As you contemplate, picture yourself standing before a long arched door—key in hand. If you're able to achieve a moment of lucidity while you dream, try to recall this image: you, the key, and the door. Picture yourself putting the key in the lock and turning it.

What does this open door reveal? Maybe it is a fancifully decorated room, an enclosed garden, or a staircase leaving up or down to someplace else. Let your dream take it from there with the assurance you'll see something new and worthwhile. Even if the dream doesn't get interesting, you'll still have made some of your own luck. It is widely agreed that "to dream of a key is a good sign."

Goddess Animal Totems

······

by Janina Renée

Many types of animals have been manifestations, totems, or symbols of the Great Goddess at one time or another. The qualities we identify with the goddess, and perceive or project into animals, can represent aspects of our inner natures. By understanding the totemic essence of an animal (or our own perception thereof), we can also relate to our own personal goddess archetypes. Integrating the lessons of the goddess's animal totems enables us to contact our instincts and portions of the deeper levels of the psyche.

The role of the life-giving mother as lady of the beasts has been recognized since times most ancient. Thus, virtually any living creature is her totem. However, the following are a few of her more familiar totems. (*Note:* Even though many of the following religious beliefs were long ago abandoned, I write in the present tense because goddesses can be active as archetypes, and also because many forgotten goddess names are being rediscovered and reactivated by Neopagans.)

Bear: Symbolically, the bear is associated with mothering and childbirth. Bear hugs and teddy bears suggest the nurturing qualities of mama bears. However, the bear also represents the aggressive and protective instincts of the mother, instinct that can invoke primal rage and fury. The bear's hibernation connects it with earth mysteries as well as the psychological quality of introspection that brings self-renewal. The Celtic goddess Artio has been associated with a bear cult and presides over wildlife in general. Freya may have been associated with bears before cats became better known in Europe. Artemis can take the form of a bear, and some of her rites have featured bear-masked dancers. Bear-goddess figures are also found in Baltic and Slavic Pagan cultures.

Bees, Beetles, and other Winged Insects: The efficient matriarchal organization of bees has long attracted interest. Folklorist Jacob Grimm said, "It seems natural, in connection with these bustling winged creatures, to think of the silent race of elves and dwarfs, which like them obeys a queen." The Roman goddess Mellona and the Lithuanian Austheia are associated with bees, and priestesses of Artemis have been called *Melissae*, which means "bees." Bees and other helpful insects are harbingers of spring and of the earth's fertility. Many have the name "Mary" or "Lady" attached to them, showing their connection with earlier goddesses. The ladybug has been an emblem of the Roman goddess Lucina and is sacred to Freya.

Birds: In folk belief, the soul is often represented as a bird, and birds can be spirits messengers. Birds symbolize thought, imagination, inspiration, intuition, and the transcendental qualities that allow the individual the personal freedom to fly beyond limitations and penetrate the higher realms. Bird imagery associated with manifestations of the goddess dates back to Paleolithic cultures. More information on bird totems follows under separate categories.

Birds of Prey: Birds of prey herald the goddess as death wielder. Freya and Frigga take on the plumage of hawks and falcons, and the sparrowhawk has been sacred to the Bohemians. The swiftness, power, and keenness of vision of these birds invokes awe and inspiration.

Cat: The comfort-seeking ways of cats associate them with Bast and Freya, goddesses of love and patronesses of all arts and pleasures. Freya also teaches witchcraft, as does Diana, who takes the form of a cat in witch lore. Cats figure in the witch lore of the Basques, and are tied in with their cult of Saint Agato. Cats' keen night vision and their rounded eyes, which are said to be roundest at the full moon, give them lunar associations. Other goddesses connected with cats are Cerridwen and Anu, and there seems to have been an oracular cat cult in Ireland. As there were no cats in Neolithic or Copper Age Europe, many of their goddess associations are more recent.

Cow: The cow is connected with the very earthy aspect of the goddess that related to the physical conditions of existence. In the Eddas, the cow Audumbla is a primal ancestress and world mother. The cow's sacred meanings are also tied in with the wealth of the earth and the fertility cycles of the moon. Goddesses associated with cows include the Hindu Lakshmi; Io and the cow-eyed Hera; Europa, who may have been a Cretan mother goddess and moon goddess; the pre-Biblical Ashtaroth; the Egyptian goddesses Isis and Hathor; and the Celtic Brigid, who is said to have been a cowherd.

Crow and Raven: These birds have been manifestations of the death goddess. The Celtic war goddess called the Morrigan appears on the battlefield in the guise of a crow or raven, and combines aspects of the goddesses Ana, Badb, and Macha. The Baltic goddess Ragana also has totemic associations with crows.

Deer: The tender relationships between does and their fawns make us see them as primal mother figures, and the deer has been a totem of the birth-giving goddess since early times. Artemis can take the form of a deer, and the deer also has Sumerian goddess associations. As we become aware of the importance of healing touch, the gentleness of the doe can take on special meanings for us.

Dog: Dogs are important household guardians, and mythological dogs are companions of the dead and guardians of the underworld in Egyptian, Greek, Mexican, and Northern European lore. Their nocturnal howling makes them heralds of the death goddess. One of Hecate's three heads is described as dog-like. Dog symbolism is also associated with Hel, Artemis, and Nehalenna.

Dove: The dove is a manifestation of the fertility goddesses of Asia Minor, India, Crete, Greece, and Northern Europe. Harke, a form of Freya or Holda, flies through the air in the shape of a dove in order to make the earth fruitful. Also associated with doves are Atargatis, Tanith the Carthaginian goddess of heaven (who is accompanied by two of them), Venus, and Hera.

Fish and Sea Mammals: The watery realm is likened to the greater unconscious and engenders and nourishes life. Because fish move through this element, they symbolize fertility and richness as well as the psychological process of "becoming." An ancient Boetian amphora shows the goddess with a fish in her womb. The fish also represents deep emotions. Among goddesses associated with fish symbolism are Atargatis the Syrian "fish mother," Artemis, Aphanian, Dictynna the "lady of the nets," Britomartis, Sedna the Eskimo heroine who rules an undersea realm and engendered whales and seals, Venus, Myrrhine, Mara, Hecate, and Behrta.

Frogs, Toads, and Other Aquatic Creatures: Aquatic creatures share symbolism with fish. Frogs represent embryonic life, due to their stages of transformation. In folklore, the sounds of frogs bring the rains and the return of spring. A frog goddess is a characteristic motif in early Anatolia, and the Egyptian frog-headed goddess Heket gave breath to humans at the time of creation. Toad figurines have been used as fertility charms, and toads appear as witches' familiars, and are the main manifestation of the Baltic witch goddess Ragana.

Horse: Horses represent personal power, both in physical and spiritual domains. The horse is one of the most favored totems in shamanic rites, carrying its rider into other dimensions. The horse is especially an emblem of Celtic goddesses, including Rigantona, Epona, Etain, and Macha. Hecate is depicted with the head of a horse, and Demeter disguised herself as a mare.

Lioness: Big cats suggest the terrifying yet beautiful aspects of the dark goddess because they have great power coupled with grace. The lioness depicts the raw power and destructive fury of the goddess. Thus, the gentle cow goddess Hathor could transform into Sekhmet the lioness, saying "For truly, when I spill men's blood, my heart rejoices." The lioness also has symbolic affinities to the fire element. Astarte has been depicted with the head of a lioness, and Erishkegal and Bast are also able to make that transformation. Tibetan Tara and the fierce Hindu goddess Durga are shown mounted on lions. Other goddesses accompanied by lions include Cybele and Fortuna.

Owl: Folk belief gives owls prophetic knowledge of human destiny, but also makes them birds of ill omen. Owls are emblems of Athena, goddess of wisdom. They are also manifestations of the death goddess. Owl-goddess figurines were important funeral objects through Neolithic and Megalithic times. The owl was the hieroglyph for death in ancient Egypt. The owl retains her death goddess image in the Northern European legends wherein a nun is transformed into an owl and flies before the Wild Hunt, acting as Odin's herald. This is probably related to the legend of Blodeuwedd, who is transformed into an owl and pursued by Gwydion, Odin's Celtic counterpart. Signifying both wisdom and death, owls illustrate the ambivalent nature of the crone aspect of the goddess.

Rabbit and Hare: Though they are biologically different, rabbits and hares share some symbolism. Their sex drive and reproductive capacity is legendary. The fact that rabbits are burrowing animals connects them with the earth mysteries, and hares have traditional associations with the moon in both eastern and western lore. Shape-shifting witches favored the forms of hares, connecting them with the goddess Sorcery. As symbols of the earth's renewal, bunnies are sacred to Ostara. These creatures are also sacred to Venus, Diana, and Hecate.

Serpent: Because snakes shed their skin, they signify self-renewal and immortality. Snakes also personify the life force, as their coiling forms suggest energy flow. Geomancers perceive the earth's energy taking a serpentine course as it flows through landforms. Snakes are tied to the earth mysteries, and their stirring in spring suggests the quickening of nature. Minoan goddess or priestess figurines clutching snakes are admired art objects. Serpent effigies have been cult objects associated with Brigid, whose domination of life energies makes her patroness of healing arts. One of Hecate's heads is serpentine. Coatlicue the five-fold goddess of the Aztecs is serpent-skirted, and Ix-Chel, Mayan goddess of water, the moon, childbirth, and weaving also has snake symbolism. Snake goddess figurines in household shrines of old Europe show her as household guardian. Other goddesses depicted as handling serpents or having them as totems include Rhea, Athena, Demeter, Hera, Britomartis, and Brehkina.

Spider: Spider symbolism shows the goddess as the matrix of life, binding all destinies together. This is evident in the descriptions of the Mayan goddess Ix-Chel, called Lady-Unique-All-Embracing, and of whom it is said that the world is her web and she is at its center. Spider Grandmother is important in southwestern lore. To the Zuni and Hopi she is an earth goddess and mother of the twin war gods. To the Kiowa she is a culture heroine who continues to help her people. The spider also appears as a benevolent figure in Ukrainian folklore.

Sow: The sow represents two very different aspects of the goddess. Her fast-growing, rounded body symbolizes pregnancy and the earth's fertility. Representations of the sow as grain goddess date to the seventh millennium BCE. It's good luck to exchange pig figurines on New Year's Day, and pig-shaped cookies were sacrificial offerings. On the other hand, swine have a reputation for eating any of their young that are flawed. This is a dark aspect of nature, who is not a doting mother and does not tolerate weakness or incompetence. The sow is a prime manifestation of the white goddess, whose names include Demeter, Cerridwen, Henwen, and Freya.

Waterbirds: Because of the richness of marshes, rivers, and ponds in engendering life, the birds and animals dwelling in them symbolize fertility and transformation. Thus we have a belief that the stork brings babies. Waterbirds were significant to goddess worship early on, and anthropomorphic waterbird figures from the Upper Paleolithic attest to this. Diving birds also symbolize unconscious knowledge because of their ability to penetrate the depths. Swans are seen to glide between the worlds and are symbols of Brigid in Gaelic Scotland, and Norns and Valkyries often take their forms. Swans are also sacred to Venus, as are ducks.

Wolf: For the Romans, the she-wolf was a primal ancestress, having nursed the founders of their great city. The howling of wolves associates them with the moon and death goddesses, such as Diana, Hecate, and Hel. In Scandinavian lore, sorceresses ride wolves, and old women living alone in the forest are called "wolf mothers" and give shelter to wolves when they are hunted.

How to Communicate
with Your Pet

......

by Marguerite Elsbeth

The animal companions we choose as pets have much to teach us, and we have a lot to learn, especially in the way of communication. I knew of a family who had a pot-bellied pig named Taylor. Usually Taylor was well-behaved, but every time Grandpa Jones came for a visit, Taylor would do something nasty on the living room rug. Close communication revealed that Taylor resented Grandpa referring to him as "Porkchop." In fact, the pig knew exactly what Grandpa had in mind, because Grandpa visualized juicy, succulent porkchops every time he called Taylor by that name. Obviously Taylor was threatened and angered by Grandpa's rude mental imagery.

Pet Talk

Animals are psychic. Because they are primarily feeling creatures and spend so much time dreaming, they are accustomed
to think in pictures. Therefore, in order to communicate with
your pet, you must learn to increase your ability to transmit and
receive mental images so that you can fulfill your pet's wants and
needs as well as your own.

First, "bone" up on your own innate super-sensory abilities.
Gaze at a candle flame. Hold an image in your mind, such as a
cube or circle. Now, watch for certain telling signs that your pet
needs to talk. For example, if Hairball, your beloved cat, takes
to sitting on your head every time your friends come over, she
may be jealous, cold, lonely, or simply letting you know that her
glorious pelt is far more attractive than your new hairdo. Or,
should Puddles the pooch not respond when you call his name,
he may (a) want a bribe, or (b) want a new name.

Finally, once you have determined that something unusual
is happening with your pet, try the following: Catch your pet's
attention. Look into his or her eyes. Leave your mind blank to receive an image. Fashion a response image and send it to your pet.

Trust me. With a lot of patience and a little practice, you
and your pet will be communicating beyond words in no time!

The Raven

......

by Marguerite Elsbeth

Ravens belong to the bird family called *Corvidae:* large, omnivorous, gregarious, and obnoxious. These black birds can't sing worth a lick, though their raucous language is quite communicative and extensive. Live food doesn't interest ravens; they prefer dead things, like roadkill and other birds' eggs. In fact, ravens hold funerals for their dead. One bird will guard the body and rattle a death song, letting the other ravens know what has occurred. They form a circle around the corpse and dance round and round, croaking softly from deep within their throats. For this reason, the ancient Celts and other tribal peoples associated the raven with death goddesses. Considering the habits of this bird, it is easy to derive other attributions also.

- The black-feathered raven calls to mind the beginning, the maternal night, the primordial darkness, and vital primal earth.

- Soaring through the sky in graceful, rag-winged flight, the raven is a messenger heralding transformation and change.

- Some Native American tribes believe the raven to have the powers of attention, observation, swiftness, and ambivalence, as well as the ability to find lost objects.

- Celtic and Germanic tribes, as well as Native American and Siberian peoples, once believed the raven to be the creator of the visible world.

- Contemporary tribal people the world over still associate the raven with magic, believing that through its spirit one can divine the future.

- In Celtic myth, the raven was one of the most important symbols of the terrible mother, for the raven is a scavenger that devours corpses on the battlefield. Fighting Celts would find ravens eating at the rotting flesh of the dead warriors, adding to the bird's mystique as guardian spirit of the dead.

- The raven eating the desiccated remains of the body is an earthy symbol of the Celtic goddesses Badb and the Morrigan, who, like the Aztec goddess called Filth-eater the witch, consume all misconceptions lingering in our souls.

- The Celtic goddess Blodeuwedd; Freya and Holda of Norse myth; and Rhea and Artemis in the Mediterranean are often depicted as sorceresses—black-faced and long-haired, with a raven flying above them.

- The Scottish witch Isobel Gowdie testified that she often left her body and traveled in the shape of a raven to otherworldly realms.

- The Irish banshee, or "woman of the hills," is often imaged as a raven, for she is heard moaning and keening whenever death is near.

- Sometimes the raven is a white goddess of death and rebirth: the ancient European queen of the dead. The white lady, as she is sometimes called, may be seen dressed in black when she comes forth as a raven to gather the souls of the dead. The Celtic love goddess Branwen's name means "white raven."

- The Pueblo tribe of New Mexico says that one day, a long way back, ravens had white feathers and could speak like humans. E-ye-e-co, the mother of life, told the ravens to stop picking the eyes out of dead people or they would be punished. One raven couldn't resist this tasty treat and picked out the eye of a dead person anyway. At that moment, all the ravens turned black and lost their ability to speak.

Guardian Animal
Archetypes

......

by Sandra Kynes

Since ancient times, people have recognized the power of certain animals and invoked their spirits during ritual. Many deities, both male and female, are associated with particular animals, which also act as their earthly representatives. From prehistoric times through classical Greece, people have revered and feared certain animals. In cases such as the snake, an animal honored by one culture was deliberately made evil by another to subvert and control people's belief systems.

In modern Pagan practice it is not unusual to look to an animal for guidance and protection because of its association with a particular tradition or deity. Guardian animals serve to protect the turnings of the cycle of the year as well as one's life. There are four in particular whose history and association with ritual date back to prehistoric times.

Animal	Attributes	Archetypes	Function	Direction
Bear	Sustainer, nurturer	Life giver, mother	Life	North
Owl	Seer, wisdom	Death wielder, crone	Death	East
Snake	Mover, changer	Transformer, maiden	Rebirth	West
Bull	Vitality, life	Male, the god	Spark of life	South

The Bear: Mother Goddess

The mother aspect of the goddess not only encompassed giving birth but also provided sustenance and protection. For ancient as well as modern people, the bear is a symbol of power. Less today than in earlier times, the bear's power was perceived as the she-bear protective mother.

The bear was one of the animals that symbolized the goddess's various functions. Bear-shaped pottery was produced continuously from 7000 to 3000 BCE in a wide area from western Ukraine, throughout the Balkan Peninsula, Greece, and the Lipari Islands north of Sicily. Both the shape and the function of these vessels served as symbols. The bear is one of the symbolic animals of Artemis/Diana and is also linked to childbirth.

Just as the bear hibernates, winter is a time for us to slow down and turn inward to do our self-work. We then emerge in the spring with renewed spirit. As the guardian of the north,

Bear helps us nurture ourselves and find the strength of the protective mother within no matter what our gender.

The Owl: Death Wielder

One aspect of the ancient bird goddess hybrid was that of death wielder. She was portrayed as a bird of prey: owl, vulture, crow, or raven. She was the one with wisdom who prepared people for death and eventual rebirth. In later mythology, this aspect was turned into the hag—a fearful being who brought about a horrid death. But to the owl goddess and those who believed in her, death was not seen as a mournful end of life, but rather a passage in the cycle of life, death, and rebirth.

Representations of owls and owl goddesses have been found on pottery in tombs marked with symbols of life and regeneration. These have been found in a wide area and time frame: Syria (8000 to 7000 BCE); Newgrange, Ireland (3200 BCE), and Folkton, England (2000 BCE).

The owl's association with the goddess survived into Greek culture in representations of Athena. Homer even referred to her as the owl-eyed goddess. In our present-day culture, the owl symbolizes knowledge and is frequently depicted wearing a graduate's mortarboard, although it is no longer connected with the goddess or her wisdom.

For Pagans, the owl that glides silently through the air is a reminder of the dark power of the goddess. Although a creature of the night, owl as guardian of the east will carry us from darkness (or the womb and tomb) into the light of a new day (rebirth).

The Snake: Transformer

Since the Paleolithic period, wavy meandering lines represented water, snakes, and the life force combined into one. This symbol of fecundity was often linked to Tiamat, Babylonian goddess of salt water, and Mesopotamian Inanna/Ishtar and Ua Zit who was the patron deity of predynastic lower Egypt. The snake goddess of Crete (2000 to 1700 BCE) nurtured the world with life-giving moisture. Various versions of the snake goddess continued to appear well into the time of historical Greece.

The snake goes through obvious cyclical changes, as do women, the moon, and the seasons. The snake is symbolic of the goddess as maiden. Maidenhood is a time of transformation, when a child becomes a woman whose moisture is capable of bringing forth new life. Likewise, boys experience powerful transformations as they enter manhood.

In spite of being turned into a symbol of creeping evil thought to be responsible for the downfall of humankind in the Garden of Eden, the positive power of the snake has managed to survive. In ancient Greece, Asklepios and his daughter Hygeia were healers who were depicted with a staff around which snakes coiled. This has been carried over into our modern medical symbol, the caduceus.

Powerful transformation takes place in the form of spiritual awakening, as well as the change of maiden into woman, and boy into man. Growth of body and spirit are integral parts of the life cycle. As guardian of the west, Snake helps us navigate the transformative stages that occur at puberty and throughout our lives.

The Bull: The God

Horned gods Cernunnos, Herne, and Pan represent powerful male qualities that run deeper than the stereotypical idea of brute strength. Along with a depiction of the full moon (the goddess in her full mother aspect), a set of horns represents the moon's waxing and waning phases. Together, this male and female energy represents completeness.

In the depths of the cave at Lascaux, France (15000 to 10000 BCE), bulls depict vital life energy. In many ancient cultures, fast-growing horns were symbolic of regeneration.

Stylized horns of consecration have been found in the Temple of Knossos on Crete (2000 to 1600 BCE) and at Vinca and Karanova on the Balkan Peninsula (5000 to 4000 BCE). In later Greek mythology and European folklore, Zeus and river gods were portrayed as bulls.

While the goddess is life giver and death wielder, the God represents the essence of what is born and destroyed. He is the cycle. The Sun King born at Winter Solstice begins to decline at Summer Solstice. He is cut down with the harvest to sleep in the goddess's womb until he is reborn. As guardian of the south, Bull (the God) carries the fiery spark that keeps the cycle of life turning.

In Ritual

The power of these guardian animals can be evoked in ritual and around your home as ongoing reminders of the cycles you live. The owl (death wielder) in the east, combined with the snake (transformer) in the west, symbolize the passing of days and lifetimes—dark to light and light into darkness. It is an endless circle of time and timelessness. The bear (mother goddess) in the north and the bull (father god) in the south provide an axis on which female and male energies are balanced.

The flow of life spirals forever in past and future.

The Magical
Emergency Kit

......

by John Michael Greer

One important lesson of the mysteries is that the magical realms have their dangers and pitfalls as well as their blessings. This is a lesson, unfortunately, that too many novice magicians learn the hard way.

As magical practitioners have known since ancient times, the parts of the universe we encounter with the magical senses are every bit as diverse as the parts we encounter with our physical sense. If you visit another city, for example, you may encounter lovers, friends, strangers, muggers, and politicians; if you go hiding in a forest, you may meet mosquitoes and skunks as well as deer and singing birds. In the same way, the universe of magic is inhabited by a vast range of beings and forces. Some of these may be friends to you, others may be hostile, and still others won't be interested in you at all. In other words, the human voyagers you encounter in your magical journeys will be of many different sorts, and not all of them may be friendly or trustworthy.

Dealing effectively with potential trouble in magic is not necessarily a simple matter. Good intentions will help, but they're not enough by themselves. Accurate information, which can be learned from books, from other magical practitioners, or from your own experience, is a good deal more useful.

Furthermore, there are several items of use in your magical journey. As in any journey, you need a good street map, a few coins for phone calls, and a bottle of pepper spray to help you navigate your way through a modern city; or some insect repellent, rain gear, and good hiking boots in the forest. In the same way, certain pieces of magical equipment will help get you through the rough places in the realms of inner experience.

In fact, it can be useful to assemble these things in a magical emergency kit, which can be packed into a convenient box or shoulder bag, kept in or near the room where you do most of your personal magical work, and carried with you when you attend group workings or festivals. That way, your protective and guiding tools can be used in the event of psychic or magical attack, when a ritual goes awry, or at any other time when magical energies become disrupted or unbalanced.

To some extent, the contents of your magical emergency kit will depend on the tradition of magic you practice, and on the skill and experience you've developed in it. Much will also depend on your own strengths and weaknesses. Still, the following items should probably find a place in your kit.

- A steel-bladed athame, ritual dagger, or trident. Most systems of Western magic make us of the subtle-energy effects of iron and steel for protecting against hostile or disruptive energies. Whatever specific tool your tradition uses for these purposes, one should be part of your kit. It should be ritually consecrated and kept wrapped in silk or linen to protect it.

- A portable censer, charcoal, waterproof matches, and a folding fan. Incense is one of the most useful tools in any magical emergency. Having these items ready will ensure that you can use the incense in any situation. The fan directs the incense smoke where it's needed.

- Blessing incense. The actual type will vary somewhat depending on your tradition, but frankincense is nearly always a good bet. Rosemary, sage, and vervain are also common. All incense should be kept in airtight containers.

- Banishing incense. Again, your choices should be guided by the type of magic you practice. Cedarwood, mugwort, and myrrh are generally good options.

- Red oil. This is an ancient bit of natural magic well worth brining back into common use. Take a cup or more of St. John's wort flowers, as fresh as possible, and put them in a clear glass jar; pour in olive oil while stirring, until the oil just covers the flowers. Put in a place where the jar will receive direct sunlight for at least a few hours each day, and let stand for two to four months. If the flowers are fresh, the oil will turn blood-red. Strain and store the oil in a cool, dark place. A drop of red oil rubbed onto the forehead will banish disruptive energies and help restore peace even in the most trying times.

- Salt. Many magical traditions use this to purify and banish. Good quality kosher salt or sea salt are best.

- A small bowl or cup, and a sealed container of incense ash. These, together with salt and clean water, can be used to consecrate holy water for use in blessings and purifications. Purl the water into the cup or bowl, and add a pinch of salt and ash. Then hold both your hands over the water and speak an appropriate blessing, concentrating on your intention. Holy water can be sprinkled around the edge of a circle to purify it. Any left over at the end of a working should be poured onto the earth.

- Protective talisman or amulets. Different schools of magic have different versions of these common tools, ranging from the little bags of herbs and graveyard dust to pasteboard disks covered with geometrical diagrams and Hebrew letters. Whatever the details, something of the sort is well worth having in your kit—kept in silk or linen to keep its charge at full intensity.

These objects, plus any other items you may choose to add to the collection, will give you options in more of the difficult situation that come up in magical work. The best kit in the world, though, will be useless if you do not know what to do with it. Take the time to make sure you know how to use every item in your kit. If any of the items are meant to be used in ritual workings, the ritual should be memorized and frequently practiced before you have to rely on it.

Magic Wands

······

BY RAYMOND BUCKLAND AND SCOTT CUNNINGHAM

Magic wands, in one form or another, are found going back to earlier time, in all civilizations. They are not only a symbol of power but also a very real means of administering that power.

Shamans, Native American medicine men, obeah men of Africa, ancient Egyptians, Druids, priests, rulers, wise men ... all have borne the magical staff or scepter, which is the magical wand of power. Even the caduceus, the physician's serpent-entwined rod, was such a tool.

According to the old grimoires, the books of magic, only certain woods may be used for making wands. Hazel wood was a favorite, though the Druids preferred yew, rowan, or hawthorn. The length would vary. Some magicians state that the length of the wand had to equal the distance from the magician's elbow to the tip of his longest finger. Others just said a standard length of 21 inches was fine. Yet for the shamans and medicine men and others, a tall staff—frequently the height of its owner—is the "correct" size!

Some wands are drilled lengthwise and an iron or copper rod is inserted. Others have crystals of various types attached to the end(s). Some are decorated with inlaid silver, carved with mystic signs and symbols, but others are starkly plain.

From all the above it might be assumed that there is nothing special about a wand itself, other than what the owner puts into it. This is true. As with all magic, what you truly believe has great bearing on how effective your magic is. If you believe that a wand must be 21 inches in length, then one measuring 22 inches will not work.

Before starting to make a wand, it is a good idea to sit down with a piece of paper and pencil and list all the requirements that you think should be there. And most importantly, have a good reason for what you list. In other words, don't insist on a purple wand just because you believe that all witches (or whoever) have purple wands! Have a purple wand because purple means something special to you in connection to the wand.

List the type of wood you need, its length and cross-section—can it be machined dowel or must it be a natural branch? What thickness? Should it be tapered? If it is natural wood, will you leave the bark on or strip it off? Should you, perhaps, cover it entirely with leather? Will the wood be left in its natural color or stained/painted/polished? Symbols can be cut into it or burned into the wood. But do you want symbols, and, if so, which ones and why?

If you fancy crystals on the wand, either at the end(s) or along the length, decide which type(s) and again, why. A fluorite at the base and a double-terminated quartz at the tip might look fine, but is that the right combination for you? The chiefs of Clan Donnachaidh in Scotland have an amulet known as Clach na Bratach. It is a chunk of quartz crystal that was found in a clump of earth that stuck to their banner when they pulled it out of the ground at Bannockburn. For years it was carried attached to the end of the standard.

Do you need a connection between the base (where you hold the wand) and the tip? If you feel you do, should it be a rod that is inserted throughout the length of the wand or should it be, say, copper wire that is wound along the outer length? If the latter, should it wind clockwise or counterclockwise?

It can be seen that the making of a wand is, indeed, a very personal thing. Or should be. A wand is a storer of energy—a capacitor. It is also a projector. It will send out that energy when you direct it and where you direct it. It is a powerful magical tool and, as such, deserves a great deal of thought where its construction is concerned. Give it that thought.

FAIRIES

......

BY SILVER RAVENWOLF

Reality? Tradition? Lore? The kingdoms and populace of fairy-enchantment have long haunted imaginations of poets, dreamers, peasants, and scholars. Most fairy mythology indicates that fairies manifest as preternatural creatures living between the worlds. This gives them the ability to sneak through the human populace unseen when they choose or blatantly appear in a variety of ways to serve their purposes if they so desire. Much like humans, members of the fairy realms have a checkered history when it comes to helping or harming those of us on the material plane.

The majority of fairy folk find their roots in European folklore, although legends and lore of similar entities circulate through most of human history, regardless of religious belief, cultural nuances, or socioeconomic status. From Eskimos to the Japanese, the tales, antics, and dangers of the "little folk" persist. The belief in fairies appears linked to the same area of human consciousness that creates a connection between religious mythos and metaphysical practices.

Through the tumultuous history of humankind, the origin of fairies has been hotly debated. Are they spirits of the dead? Fallen angels? The essence of plant and tree energy? Do they resemble humans only because we want them to, or can they really manifest in pseudo-human form? Are they lore-remnants of a race of people who have long since merged with the dust of our ever-changing planet, or is our belief in them so strong that we have actually manifested them into the astral through our own process of thought creation? Is that crazy woman walking down the street and muttering to herself as she adjusts her red hat just an odd lady or is she a redcap? Sagas and legends evolve from traditional stories, that although containing fictional and imaginative elements, may have a historical basis. These sagas and legends could represent in the popular memory a real happening that was extraordinary enough to be remembered and embellished. Perhaps our fairies fit the profile of the saga or legend?

Fairy legend doesn't just revolve around cute little people with gossamer wings or the helpful brownie. A compendium of fairy lore paints them, if not as downright malicious, with at least little regard for human morality. At best, quite a few legends portray the fairy population with prankster mentality. The most powerful and unpredictable personalities manifest as the sidhe. Originally the word *sidhe* meant mound or hill, or the dwelling of the DeDanaan after their defeat by the Milesians. These ancient shining ones, thus exiled underground, became part of folk legend, metamorphosing into the fairies as sidhe, the people of the hills. The traditional characteristics of fairies can be found in European literature as in Shakespeare's *A Midsummer Night's Dream* and *Romeo and Juliet* (in Mercutio's "Queen Mab" speech), and other great works. To escape the magics of the most dangerous fairies, one would employ the use of iron, as this metal destroys all fairy magic. The majority of fairies appear to live in some sort of organized society, whether it be the ubiquitous fairyland or underground in the mythical terrain of the sidhe. Whatever the fairy society, two facts appear to remain constant: the absence of sickness and the absence of time.

If one wishes to contact the fairies or receive their blessings, a customary offering of milk and honey should be left by the back door of your home on the first day of spring. Then, as the days warm and the world around you comes alive with the energy of manifestation, you should take walks around your home or spend time meditating outdoors, sending loving energy to the area. As your thoughts merge with the universal consciousness, you will be sending the signal that you come in peace, merging the spirit of yourself with the energy patterns of the land.

References

Ellis, Peter Berresford. *A Dictionary of Irish Mythology*. Oxford Paperback Reference. Oxford University Press, 1987.

Evans-Wentz, W. Y. *The Fairy Faith in Celtic Countries*. Library of the Mystic Arts. Citadel Press, 1990.

Mercatante, Anthony. *The Facts on File Encyclopedia of World Mythology and Legend*. Facts on File, 1988.

MUSIC IN RITUAL

......

by Reverend Gina Pace

Right from the start, I'd like to explain that while it is a valid topic in its own right, using recorded music as background material during a ritual is not my intended topic here. Many people like to play recorded music during a ritual, and I myself have done so on several occasions—with good results. However, what I'm discussing in this article is the use of music within the ritual structure itself.

Having been raised Catholic, song and music were always considered an integral part of my early religious upbringing. The priest would often sing various parts of the Mass, with the congregation singing in response to him. I can honestly say that I have always felt that the Mass seemed a little more "special" or "sacred" when the parts were sung.

There are several intervals in which songs are also inserted. This is also true of other mainstream Christian services, as well as other religious services. I remember a music teacher of mine back in sixth grade who always used to say that singing was praying twice. I guess it's a belief that stuck.

There is no need to feel musically perfect or superior when offering one's ritual to the God and Goddess. I think it's safe to say, if they gave you a voice, they'd rather you lift it up in prayer to them than feel embarrassed that you can't carry a tune as well as you'd like. After all, freeform singing is not a precise talent. Priests in churches don't dwell on how they sound. Nor do you have to feel as though you are being judged. Lift your voice up and don't be afraid to use it.

Another way of using music in ritual is to use various instruments to symbolize, call upon, or simulate the different elements for the circle. When I am working a ritual circle, I always begin by calling the four elements to witness the ritual. This does not have to be a terribly formal event. In fact, you can do it without saying a word if you use musical instruments to bring in each element. Let's say, for example, you wish to open your circle by calling in the element of air. A woodwind instrument, such as a flute, can represent air. There are many types of indigenous native flutes available, pan flutes, zen flutes, and cedar flutes among these. I use a tin penny whistle, which is in an old Irish favorite that I bought many years ago at a local music store for about five dollars. The memories alone make it a worthwhile addition to ritual. And its close affiliation with air makes it a perfect instrument with which to summon the element to the circle.

I begin in the east corner, which belongs to air, and I move slowly about the ritual space in a clockwise or sunwise, direction, playing my flute in a freeform manner. It tends to have an eerie kind of sound that adds to the ambience of the ritual. When I have completely the circle, I place the flute in the eastern corner, and move to the southern corner to call the next element, fire.

It is more difficult to come with a good instrument for the element of fire. I thought of the various traits of fire—passion, excitement, energy, momentum, ambition, and joy—and I chose a pair of Mexican maracas that I found on eBay. They are elaborately carved out of a pair of gourds. Many different native traditions have similar instruments. Shaking a pair of maracas has a primitive feeling of passion and joy to it that fits perfectly with the fire element. I begin in the southern corner of the circle and again, moving clockwise through the circle, shake my maracas, and welcome in the passion of fire. When I am back to the south again, I place them down and move to the west.

The west represents the element of water, which for me is a softer, emotionally nurturing element—so its instrument will have a softer, gentler sound. I have always associated the sound of bells and chimes with water, so I use a Tibetan singing bell, which is a handheld bronze bell that comes with a wooden wand (as opposed to a clapper). Or those who have never seen a singing bell before, it works like a singing bowl, only you hold the bell and you rub the wand around the edge of it and the bell's song becomes louder and louder as you continue. Its song will eventually fill the room with a pure sound that is less jarring than if you rang the bell. I walk with the bell slowly as I make it sing along the entire circumference of the circle, and then place it back in the west when I am done. Finally, I move to the north.

The north corner is the home of the element of earth. This is also a nurturing energy, but in a grounding, growing sense. I like to use a drum for the earth that is made with a natural skin head and a carved wooden body. The style of drum you use is not important, but you should feel comfortable walking around with it. Mine is an African djembe that has a somewhat hourglass-shaped body. Any kind of drum works, as long as you feel a kinship with it. Again, beginning in the north corner, and moving clockwise, I drum the entire circle round, coming to a stop in the north again. There, I set the drum down. I am now ready to begin my ritual.

Many people like to use their instruments during the ritual itself. I find this a bit cumbersome unless you are doing a group ritual. In that case, you would have four people chosen to each represent an element, and each stop described above would be carried out by its respective person in turn. During the ritual itself, each person may play their instrument when the element is invoked. Whenever my circle meets to do a ritual, we have a period of time when we each reflect deeply on what we are grateful for in our lives, what we would like to ask for, and what we have seen come to pass that we had wished for previously. During these times, it is a wonderful thing to have the circle mates playing their instruments softly in support while you are talking about things that often become quite emotional.

After the prayers come the cakes and ale. I like to have everyone play their instruments again during this time, only this time we play more joyfully. One person will begin a rhythm, and each person will add to it until everyone is playing. This freeform music takes on a life of its own and helps to express great joy and happiness.

When I am doing my solitary ritual, I drum a single powerful rhythm at this point in the ritual, starting more slowly but gradually increasing in frequency till I feel I have released my energy properly. I always feel greatly satisfied after this.

If you have other instruments that you are interested in—a guitar, a tuba, you name it—feel free to incorporate them into your own ritual in a similar fashion. Even a piano can be used creatively. I have a friend who moves her piano into the center of the circle as the altar table, and then pounds away on it brilliantly near the end of the rite.

As with any ritual circle, when you are ready to close, reverse all your directions to release the circle. Begin by releasing earth, which you called in last. Move counterclockwise, and drum the circle round till you come back to the north, thank the earth for its energy, and release it.

Moving to the west, releasing water in a counterclockwise motion as well. Follow suit with each of the other elements until you have completed the circle.

Unleashing the
Magic of Your Aura

......

by Edain McCoy

Most magical folk are familiar with the aura, the field of light energy that surrounds the human body, and know that it can be read to determine disposition, character, or illness. What many do not know is that the aura can be temporarily programmed to reflect the color of your choosing. This is done for a variety of magical and mundane needs, such as helping alter your mood, giving you a boost of energy, or projecting a desired image to others. Even people who are not psychic, and who vehemently do not believe in the existence of the aura, unconsciously pick up on the color changes if you project them strongly enough.

To alter you auric color, close your eyes, relax, and allow yourself to feel grounded and centered. As you do this, focus on the color you want to project, then begin to feel the core of energy at the center of your being expanding as this color. Keep up this visualization for about five minutes, or until you feel that you have sufficiently colored the light field around you. The results will be temporary and, depending on how much energy you put into the act, how good you are at projecting energy, and how far you are deviating from your natural auric color, the effect should last between twenty and sixty minutes.

Red: Project red when you need a boost of energy, when you want to let off steam, or are preparing for an athletic event. Keep in mind that others may perceive a red aura as stress or anger.

Orange: Project orange to attract attention to yourself or when you need a boost of energy but do not feel you can handle the intensity of red.

Yellow: Project yellow when you need to bolster your creative self or when you are deep into intellectual pursuits, such as studying for an exam. Others who sense the yellow aura will likely view you as being very smart.

Green: Project green when you need a calming influence. The color sense will be picked up by others around you, and you may find that you not only calm yourself, but your entire environment as well. Try on a green aura when you are gardening to help you merge with the energies of the plants.

Blue: Project blue when you are attempting any spiritual pursuit or when you suffer from insomnia. Those with blue auras are perceived by others as being balanced and selfless people, impressions that make this a good color to work with when applying for a job in a service-oriented industry.

Indigo: Project this blue-violet color when attempting any psychic work. Others who perceive this color will see you as being dreamy and not completely "with it." Avoid indigo when on the job hunt or any other time when you need to appear competent.

Violet: Project violet when attempting to heal yourself or others, or when you are working with visualization to ward off a bad habit. Those who pick up on your violet aura think of you as a person of intense emotion—ever hear of a purple passion?

Pink: Project pink for peacefulness, when trying to stir up a romance, or when you wish to appear nonthreatening.

Peach: Project peach when you want to turn your attention outward to other matters. This can be useful to help overcome depression or when you need to put aside an issue for a while and let things work themselves out. Peach auras are perceived by others as being compassionate, making this a good color for health care professionals to use when dealing with difficult patients.

Brown: Project a brown aura when you are working earth magic or magic for animals. Be aware that others sense brown as being dull-witted and even untrustworthy, so avoid carrying them into the workplace or anywhere else where first impressions matter.

White: Project white when you want to go unnoticed. White appears very neutral to the psychic eye as it tends to camouflage itself against the other energy fields that surround us. It is sometimes even hard for trained psychics to pick up on white auras.

Joining a Magical Lodge

......

by John Michael Greer

Back before today's magical renaissance, most magicians in the Western world learned their art by joining a lodge. Lodges were the most common type of organization in the magical community of those times, and lodges nearly had a stranglehold on magical knowledge. It's hard to imagine from today's perspective, but between 1700 and 1900, fewer than a hundred books on practical magic were published in English, and most of the them were very hard to obtain. At a time when being openly involved in magic was a shortcut to social ostracism, too, the secrecy of magical lodges had a definite appeal.

Times have changed. Teachings that were once jealously guarded can now be found in shopping mall bookstores, and covens, circle, and other less formal groups play a much larger role in the magical community than magical lodges. The lodge system itself is poorly understood these days, and not all of those who run magical lodges have a solid grasp of how and why the system works.

Despite these changes, though, there are still good magical lodges to be found, and good reasons to consider joining them. Many lodges offer a solid education in magic, based on a tested curriculum and taught by experienced magicians. Belonging to a magical lodge also offers the chance to take part in intensive group rituals, to experience a series of initiations, and to become part of a community dedicated to serious magical work.

What is a Magical Lodge?

Few people know much about lodges these days, however, and inaccurate notions about the lodge system are common. Many of these are simple confusions between lodges and other ritual groups. A lodge is not just a coven with fancier robes and titles. Nor is it a circle, a church, a cult, or an encounter group. It's a distinct kind of organization, with its own ways of carrying out the various tasks of group work.

Perhaps the most important factor that sets lodges apart from other occult groups is the role of structure. Lodge work follows a framework of rules and procedures; each lodge officer has specific duties, and ceremonial work follows texts that are changed only in special circumstances. There's a point to this—setting up a structure and sticking to it shifts the focus of the attention from management to the magical work of the lodge.

Lodge structure has another dimension. With few exceptions, lodges have a series of levels of membership—"grades" or "degrees" in lodge jargon—and magical lodge members have to earn their way up, normally by meeting the requirements of a curriculum of training. Many lodges require members to reach a certain grade before they can hold office or take other active roles in the lodge; some require members to reach a certain grade before they can attend lodge meetings at all. This may grate on modern sensibilities, but once again, there's a point to it. Advanced magical work requires a fair degree of skill to carry off successfully, and lodge members need to demonstrate that they know what they're doing before they take part.

Obviously, then, joining a magical lodge is not for everyone. To be comfortable in a lodge, it's necessary to have some tolerance for structure and an interest in serious magical work. If these things appeal to you, though, you may find a magical lodge well worth the time and effort.

Joining a Magical Lodge

Like the old recipe for rabbit pie that begins, "First catch your rabbit," the first step in joining a magical lodge is finding one. This isn't always easy. There are active magical lodges in most North American cities of any size, but few advertise their presence. Getting in touch with one may take time and patience. If you make contacts in your local magical community and ask around, you're likely to turn up lodge connections, although those connections may want to know more about you before they start answering questions.

This brings up an important point: magical lodges are usually selective about potential members. This is partly a matter of tradition, and partly one of hard experience. Not everyone who wants to join a lodge does so for good reasons, and a lodge that opens its doors to all comers may find itself saddled with members who are more interested in playing politics or sitting on the sidelines pretending to be magicians than in doing real magical work. You may be certain that a magical lodge has much to offer you, but you need to remember that the members will be asking themselves what you have to offer the lodge.

What they will be looking for, if the lodge in question is worth anything, is evidence that your interest in magic is serious, and that you are willing to commit time and energy to the lodge and its work. If they are looking for anything else, for example, money, sexual favors, or the promotion of some pet cause, you're better off working on your own. Most lodges do ask for dues to meet hall rental and other expenses, but anything more than fifteen to twenty dollars a month is probably lining someone's pocket.

The first stage of becoming a lodge member, then, is usually a matter of coming to the notice of people who belong to the lodge, or finding information that allows you to make contact. Then a more formal process begins, in most cases with a written application followed by an interview. After the interview, the lodge will vote on your application, and if you pass the vote the next thing you'll receive is a phone call or letter letting you know when to show up for your initiation. At that point, you'll stand at the beginning of a profound, transformative, and, in every sense of the word, magical journey.

A Pendulum Divination

......

by Kristin Madden

The pendulum is one of the simplest of all divination tools. It is so easy to use that even a young child can learn. It is a simple, yet powerful method that can become as complex as you need it to be.

While beautiful pendulums may be purchased in stores, just about anything that can hang on a rope or chain may be used to make a pendulum. This eliminates the need for ornate or expensive tools. At various times, I have used a ring hung on a chain, a crystal necklace, as well as a formal, weighted pendulum.

For pendulum divination, it is a good idea at the start to limit your questions to those with "yes" or "no" answers. Be simple and specific in the wording you use. Hold the question in your mind, just as you would during a tarot spread, as you allow the pendulum to divine for you.

To begin, hold the chain and allow the pendulum to hang freely. Experiment with holding it at different lengths. A longer chain or rope will result in a slower swing than will a pendulum held closer to your hand. If you need assistance keeping your arm up or holding it steady, rest your forearm on your other arm or on a few books piled on top of each other. Be sure the pendulum is still, and take a deep breath, relaxing your body and mind. You may want to ask your spirit guides or deities for their help in this work.

Ask the pendulum to show you a "yes" answer. Take note of the motions the pendulum makes. This will usually be either a circular motion in one specific direction or a side-to-side motion. Then ask the pendulum to show you the "no" answer. This should differ from the "yes" in some obvious way. If it does not, take another deep breath and ask again. Allow enough time for your body and mind to relax so the answers can flow through you and the pendulum.

Once the responses are clear, you may ask your question. If you really want to test it, ask the same question more than once. If you cannot get a clear answer, try to rephrase the question to be more specific.

Once you have gained some success with simple yes or no responses, you might have to move up to working with pendulum charts to make the answers to additional questions even more accurate. Pendulum charts often take the form of pie charts or half circles divided into three or more pieces. You might want to create a chakra or body-mind-spirit chart to help identify the areas of your life that need attention or have some bearing on the question. The pendulum will be drawn to one area of the chart more than others. The indicating response should be determined fully before moving on to other questions.

Pendulums are also wonderful tools for diagnosing illness, injury, or energy problems. When using a pendulum for these purposes, simply hold it two or three inches over the body. Move the pendulum slowly along the body, stopping at any chakra points, joints, organs, or anywhere you believe there may be an energy imbalance. Open to your intuition and watch for any unusual pendulum motions are you move along.

Be sure to clearly identify the symbolism of the various movements a pendulum makes. This will vary with the person and the pendulum, so it is a good idea to make this clear each time you use one. A good beginning is to ask what motion will indicate a "yes" and a "no." For healing work, you may want to identify the motion for imbalance, block, injury, and other disorders.

It is important to keep it simple. A pendulum can only make so many different movements, so you may want to do a general yes/no reading first, followed by a more specific one. This way a circular, clockwise motion may mean one thing in the first reading and something else in a second reading.

These same methods can be applied to divination without the presence of the person in need of assistance or healing. As usual, use the basic yes/no response for a series of questions related to the case at hand. Holding the pendulum over a photo, piece of hair or clothing, or even the person's name written on a piece of paper helps to focus the energy on the person in need. The use of one or more pendulum charts is very effective in clarifying issues or areas to explore, particularly when the individual in need is not present.

Carry your pendulum with you, play with it, and meditate with it. Do whatever you can to align your energies, and your pendulum will become a powerful tool, like any ritual object you use frequently. In your hands, it will become a conduit for spirit messages and your own intuition, allowing you to quickly and easily gain insight and answers for any life situation.

Communing with
the Triple Moons

......

BY EDAIN McCOY

The current year gives extra weight to the old phrase, "once in a blue moon." If a single solar month contains a second full moon, the second moon is said to be blue. Only one blue moon can occur in a single solar year, and in some years, may not occur at all. Modern Wiccans often say that four aspects of the self are necessary to embark on any quest: to know, to will, to dare, and to keep silent. Working with seasonal lunar triads is part of the dare. Self-examination is not easy, and only the honest seeker will discover the wisdom he or she seeks.

That is, the twelve full moons of 2005 provide us opportunity to look at our moon cycles in groupings of seasons. Through these four sets of three moons, we can see clearly see her rich symbols and the many archetypes of other triads at work—especially the wheel of the year.

The Dedicant's Triad

January 25, February 25, and March 25 are the full moons that take us from deep winter to the first days of spring. They appear when the Cailleach, the Celtic crone of winter, rules the land. Yet that same crone is the virgin goddess who gave birth to her son, the sun, at midwinter.

Connect with her energies by stretching your esbat ritual across the entire cycle of the winter moons. Stand beneath her full light and inhale the essence of dormancy, the world at rest, protected by the Celtic goddess called the Cailleach, or old woman. Know that somewhere an infant sun is waiting to emerge.

If possible, go outside and stand beneath the pale silver glow of the full moon. Stretch out your arms to embrace and welcome her. You may wish to evoke the power of this first triad by saying:

Ancient moon, encased in ice
The Cailleach blue and cold comes thrice;
Allow me to flow along your trail,
Show me the path where will prevails.

These winter moons can also serve as a focal point for personal life cycle events. During these three moons take time to meditate, looking back on your period as a dedicant, before you took formal vows of initiation. Connect the winter moons with the first three months of your studies. Think about what you've learned, how you've grown, and, if necessary, make changes in your practice and personal philosophy. Religion best serves humanity when it remained mutable and allows for change.

If you are a dedicant at this time, use this lunar energy to help you sense the subtle movements of nature and the universe. Ask it to reveal to you what you need to know as you commit to your year and a day of study.

The Initiate's Triad

April 24, May 23, and June 22 make up the second triad of full moons. They coincide with the reawakening of the planet in spring. At this time, the moon is the fertile mother, mating with her god-consort, impregnating the earth (her womb) with the harvest. June 21 is also Midsummer, the point of the sun's apex.

This period coincides with the role of the new initiate, who is now into a second year of study and has discovered that the learning, the thinking, and the questioning never stop. Paganism is not a path for those who hop from religion to religion.

An appropriate evocation for this triad might be:

The nights grow short, but the moon rides high,
Still the star of the nighttime sky;
In the moon of blood the sacred child grows,
Teach me now what I need to know.

Think back to your own initiate period. Compare how your life, thoughts, and actions changed as you continued along your path. If you are now an initiate, spend some time under these three moons meditating on how your life as in initiate differs from that of a dedicant. Ask the deities of the moon to reveal to you what you need to learn to continue growing.

The Priest's and Priestess's Triad

July 21, August 19, and September 17 take us from the verdancy of summer to the harvest. The deities are aging now. The goddess is giving birth to the abundant yield of the early autumn harvest. As the crops are gathered, each field, one by one, settles into dormancy in preparation for its winter sleep. The goddess is aging, and the sacrifice of the god-consort approaches.

This period corresponds to the priest or priestess part of the wheel of life. Whether or not you use the title, each initiated Wiccan, Witch, or Pagan is a priest or priestess, fully able to merge with and contact the deities without any intermediary.

As the fields are plowed under and the days grow shorter, reflect back on this point along your path. Bathe in the light of the harvest moons and reflect on the harvest, on growth, abundance, and dormancy. Compare these ideas to your time as priest or priestess and consider how these autumn moons have inspired or changed your life. Evoke the energy of the harvest moon with a greeting such as:

Fertile fields of gold and green,
Harbors the sacred time-between;
Her bounty grows from a single seed,
Show me the mysteries I most need.

Those who are now moving into the phase of their spiritual lives should try to connect to the energy of these three moons. Ask yourself what harvest and abundance mean in a spiritual sense. At point you should be able to connect to the lunar cycle with ease and be on to its teachings.

The Elder's Triad

The last lunar triad is October 17, November 15, and December 15. These full moons take us back into winter. The god has been sacrificed for the food of the land. The goddess mourns his loss as she prepares, as midwinter's goddess, to birth him anew. Fields lie fallow, and frost dapples to the bright orange of autumn pumpkins and squash. The last of the harvest remains to be gathered.

This final triad corresponds with the role of elder, crone, or sage. All of these are terms for Pagans who have either been practicing their faith for a long time or have taken on the tasks of extra study or of mentoring new dedicants.

This is the phase for introspection, a time to reflect on the year you have traveled and to ask for guidance in choosing the direction you want to go in the year to come.

The moons of the underworld deities contain vast knowledge, as well as the essence of our own shadow selves. It is not easy nor particularly pleasant to come face-to-face with your true self, and these moons of the waning year will not withhold their teaching if you feel ready for them.

With age comes wisdom. Allow these three moons to share their sacred wisdom with you. An example of an invocation to the moon of this triad might be:

Cold is the night and the short day brings,
The first blue frost from the Cailleach springs,
Let me gather in all the harvest I can hold,
While you share wisdom of ages untold.

Even if becoming an elder, crone, or sage is still far in your future, there is no need for you to shun the darker aspects of this deity. At first the three may appear frightening, even disturbing, but those who dare to allow themselves to be taught by the elder moons will progress rapidly along in their spiritual quests.

December 30, 2005, the last new moon of the year, makes a perfect leaping-off point to launch yourself into the cycles of time and life for not only the new lunar year, but for the solar year as well.

To the Grandmother moon of 2005 we say, "Hail and farewell, and merry must we meet again."

Fire

Modern Magic

......

BY DONALD MICHAEL KRAIG

What is Magic?

There are many systems available for improving your life. Many of the methods of achieving goals are well known: hard work, creative visualization, a positive mental attitude, prayer, getting friends or employees to work for you, etc., but before any of the above methods were developed, there was a system for achieving your goals already in existence. That ancient system has existed in various forms in all cultures. It is known as magic.

Magicians from all parts of the world have always viewed humans as having at least three aspects: the body, the mind, and the soul or spirit. (The brain is not the same as the mind. The brain is only the physical substance through which the non-material mind works on the physical plane.) All of the systems listed above use only one or two aspects of the human at best: hard work is primarily focused in the body, creative visualization is primarily in the mind, and prayer is primarily in the spirit. Magic can be the most successful system for obtaining what you desire because it is the only system that uses all three.

Like the other system, magic can be used to obtain physical plane "things," but it can also be used to help you in non-physical ways. It can help you to increase your mental abilities, improve your self-image, and increase your spirituality. All of the systems for obtaining your goals have their benefits, and all of them are good, but only magic works on all levels. Only magic is complete.

Different Styles of Magic

Over the ages, magic has developed into many different styles. These styles have been determined by the local environment and society. No system is "better" than any other; a capable magician in one will always be more successful than a poor magician following an alternate path.

But the purpose of this article is not to describe world magical systems—there isn't enough room here to cover this. Rather, I will share some thoughts on the two major magical systems of the West (especially in the US, UK, and Western Europe). The first is what is known as "natural magic." As you can tell by the name, this system is close to nature. It is practiced by people who follow the changes of Earth, the moon, and the sun, and who watch plants sprout, grow, flower, seed, and return to Mother Earth. This type of magic is practiced by witches, and it can be very powerful, very gentle, or both.

But there are many people who prefer books to herbs, temples to open sky, elaborate rituals to simple spells. The system of magic practiced by these people is known as "ceremonial magic." Again, neither natural nor ceremonial magic is better or stronger than the other. If you wish to make magic a way of life, you are urged to study both and see which feels right for you.

Natural magick is frequently simpler to perform than ceremonial magic. But for a growing number of people, the deep study of the intricacies of ceremonial magic, along with the sometimes fabulous ceremonies and ritual, is more in line with their lifestyles. The pomp and ritual of this style of magic gives them just what they want and need.

All magical systems change and evolve. The natural magic of today may be modeled after ancient rites, but it is also very new. Similarly, ceremonial magic has gone and is still going through many changes.

Modern magic is not new, nor is it composed of new versions of something old. Rather, it is an attempt to update the explanations of traditional ceremonial magic and to place those explanations into a logical and highly usable order. Modern magic is simply an explanation of what tens of thousands of people are doing today throughout the world in a way that anyone can understand. With a bit of practice, anyone can use the techniques to become a powerful magician.

The Synergy of Magic

At one time in the Western world there was a belief that the universe was a big machine that God had put into motion. This mechanistic view of the world sees every part as being just a replaceable cog in a giant machine. If the water pump in your car breaks, you get a new pump. Similarly, if you heart fails, you can now get a heart transplant.

But humans are not machines. The mechanistic view fails to account for the interrelationships between the parts, which make the human being actually greater than the sum of its parts. A single football player by himself could not play all of the positions in a game. However, backed by the rest of his team, coaching staff, trainers, etc, he can do far more than he could do alone. Just replacing a heart may not replace the cause of the heart problem—which could include poor eating habits and lack of exercise—and could result in problems developing either in the new heart or in other organs. The human being must be viewed as a whole.

As mentioned earlier, magic sees the human being as having at least three aspects: physical, mental, and spiritual. What I didn't mention is that these three aspects are connected. The subconscious mind is considered by many to be the link between the spiritual and the physical. Affect one of these aspects and you affect all three. When you use all three, you have a combination, knows as a "synergy," where the whole is greater than the sum of the parts. Magic, using all three aspects of being to improve your life, is synergistically more potent and potentially more powerful than any system that only uses one aspect of being. Magic is powerful indeed!

What Magic Isn't

Many people investigate magic, but few stay with it. The reason for this is simple—they have a false idea of what magic is. When the false expectation isn't satisfied, they leave.

Perhaps they have seen movies where demons come bubbling up from frothing, bottomless pits or watched TV's Samantha Stevens change a man into a dog by wigwagging her nose. Or perhaps you have heard the poorly written but strangely evocative prose of H.P. Lovecraft (and others) that describes the foul magics of imaginary (?) pre-human races. Or perhaps your fantasies have soared when reading Marvel Comics' *Dr. Strange*.

Sorry to disillusion you, but that isn't magic. At least it's not real magic.

Magic sets natural—not supernatural—forces into motion to help you achieve your desired goal. In this sense, magic is simply willing a change. Successful magic is having that willed change take place.

For example, if you do a ritual to obtain $50, it does not mean that an unearthly hand will drop off some crisp bills at your feet. What it means is that somebody who owes you the money may have a sudden desire to pay you back. Or perhaps someone whom you helped in the past remembered the favor and gives you a $50 gift. Or perhaps you'll receive your tax return quicker. Or maybe your boss will give you a bonus or offer you some extra work that will pay $50. Magic can make things happen, but they happen naturally. There is nothing evil here.

Sometimes magic doesn't work. It is interesting to note that if a scientist cannot duplicate an experiment, skeptics say that there was something wrong with her or her technique, but if someone's magic fails they say it is because magic doesn't work. Poppycock!

Magic works when all of the conditions are correct (including the mindset of the magician) and if the magician follows all of the scientific protocols (does the ritual properly). The magician, like the scientist, will keep a record of the experiment/ritual so that he or she can discover what was done right and what was done wrong. In this way, a magician compiles a personal magical text. In a very real sense, a magician is a spiritual scientist.

Another myth is the "magic word." Words by themselves have no magical powers. The image of a child picking up a book, poorly reading a few lines of broke Hebrew, Greek, or Latin, and summoning up a demon is only a fiction. However, when written or vocalized properly, words can affect both the physical and non-physical worlds and cause changes through our multiplaned universe.

But modern magic does not take years of study before you can become a successful magician. With just a little practice, along with the understanding of what you are doing and the techniques involved, you can do magic!

Valentine:
Your Heart's Desire

......

by Raymond Buckland and Scott Cunningham

February 14 is Valentine's Day. It was also the eve of the Roman feast of the Lupercal. In fact, Valentine's Day is descended from, and is a very watered down version of, the Lupercalia.

The feast of the Lupercal fell on the Ides of February: the fifteenth. But like all pagan feasts, its celebration was started the night before, as the moon began to rise in the sky. Goats were sacrificed at the festival to the god Faunus. Faunus was the ancient deity of wild nature and fertility. He was also regarded as a giver of oracles.

The following morning two naked young men—priests who were referred to as "he-goats"—would skin the sacrificial animals and tie girdles made from the skins about their waists. They would then run around the boundaries of the old city of Rome, on the Palatine hill, carrying with them other lengths of the goatskin in the form of whips. They would "beat the bounds." Anyone who stood in their way as they ran would also be whipped by the naked priests. To be so struck with the skin of the sacrificial animal was to be imbued with the god's fertility. It therefore became the common practice for barren women to stand along the way and hope to be struck by the priests as they ran past. In this way the women would come to conceive through the ritual flagellation.

The modern Valentine's Day owes much to its origins. The concept of becoming fertile has distilled down to declarations of love. The aspect of Faunus as a giver of oracles ties in with many of the more recent love "lotteries" of Valentine's Day. Today most people sign the cards they send their loved ones, but it used to be the fashion to send them anonymously, leaving the recipient wondering as to the identity of his/her admirer.

Henry Bourne, in his *Antiquitates Vulgares* (1725) says, "It is a ceremony, never omitted among the vulgar (common folk), to draw lots, which they term Valentines, on the eve before Valentine's Day. The names of a select number of one sex, are by an equal number of the other put into some vessel; and after that, every one draws a name, which is called their Valentine, and which is also looked upon as a good omen of their being man and wife afterwards."

In northern England and parts of Scotland is found a similar custom even today. An equal number of young men and woman write down their names on pieces of paper. The men's names are placed in one bag and the women's in another. Each then draws a name from the opposite sex's bag. In this way each has two Valentines: the one they drew and the one who drew them. If the two should happen to coincide then this is taken as an omen that marriage is in their future.

A Handfasting Ceremony

······

by Nina Lee Braden

This ceremony was written for a handfasting issuing two officials: a high priest and a high priestess. However, it can also be performed by one official. It can be used for a legal religions wedding, a non-legal religious handfasting, or for a commitment ceremony. In this ceremony, I will refer to the couple as Moonpiper and Windsong since those names are non-gender specific. It can also be adapted to reflect a more specialized spiritual path.

Casting of the Circle

High priestess. Let us recognize the sacredness of this space. All space is sacred, and all times are sacred. Let us consciously acknowledge and recognize the sacredness that exists all around us today, here, now. *(Both officials stand at the altar.)*

High priest *(walking to the east).* Let us recognize the sacredness of the east and the element of air. The breeze that caresses our cheeks is sacred. The perfume of flowers is sacred. Our very breath is sacred. Breathe and honor the sacredness of air.

(Walking to the south). Let us recognize the sacredness of the south and the element of fire. The flame that lights the candle is sacred. The fire that cooks our food is sacred. The passion in our hearts is sacred. Feel your passion, and honor the sacredness of fire.

High priestess *(walking to the west).* Let us recognize the sacredness of the west and the element of water. The salt water of the ocean is sacred. The drop of dew on the leaf is sacred. The fluids that flow through our bodies are sacred. Recognize and honor the sacredness of water.

(Walking to the north). Let us recognize the sacredness of the north and the element of earth. The ground that we walk on is sacred. The trees and mountains and sand are sacred. Our bones are sacred. Acknowledge the strength of your bones and honor the sacredness of earth. *(Both officials move to the center or altar.)*

High priestess. We ask that the Lord and Lady, the divine masculine and feminine, shine on us today and lend their love.

High priest. All days are sacred, but today is especially so. We come together today to honor the vows of love and commitment of Moonpiper and Windsong. Let us join today with joyous hearts, sending out love to Moonpiper and Windsong and to all who would welcome a gift of joy.

High priestess. Who stands in support of Moonpiper and Windsong? *(Here their friends, attendants, witnesses, or family can speak briefly or merely say "We do." You may insert a poem or*

*quotation that is a favorite of the handfast couple or one appropri-
ate to the season or to a specific spiritual tradition.)*

High priestess. What are the benefits of being handfasted?
Why should two people make a commitment to each other?

High priest. Being handfasted is not easy, even when you
are handfasted to a wonderful person. Why become handfasted?

High priestess. Because it is an opportunity for growth.
Moonpiper, in committing to Windsong, you commit to studying yourself so that you may be the best person possible. You also
commit to studying Windsong in order to help his/her growth.

Windsong, in committing to Moonpiper, you commit to
studying yourself so that you may be the best person possible.
You also commit to studying Moonpiper in order to help in
his/her grown.

High priest. You grow in self-knowledge, and you grow in
knowledge of others. You will learn to see life from others' points
of view, and your life will be enriched. Knowledge leads to wisdom and power always with love, always with responsibility.

High priestess. Handfasting is also an opportunity for worship. Through the views you make to each other and the lives that
you live together, you show your worship of the lord and lady.

High priest. Handfasting is an opportunity to establish a tradition. Through the home that you make together, you blend
your personal paths and traditions into a new tradition. In so
doing, you add to the spiritual growth of all.

High priestess. Moonpiper, do you have any words that you
want to speak to Windsong at this time? *(Here Moonpiper may
speak extemporaneously or may read from a prepared speech.)*

Windsong, so you have any words that you want to speak to Moonpiper at this time? *(Here Windsong may speak extemporaneously or may read from a prepared speech.)*

High priestess. Like the gentle breezes of the east, caress each other gently.

High priest. Like the fierce winds of the east, proclaim with power your love for one another.

High priestess. Like the warm sunlight of a summer morning, give warmth and encouragement to each other.

High priest. Like the strong sun of a summer midday, let your love shine undimmed and high overhead.

High priestess. Like the sweet rain that nurtures our souls, may you nurture one another.

High priest. Like the ocean, may your love for each other be powerful and deep, the undercurrent to all else in your lives.

High priestess. Like the fruits and vegetables of the earth, many you feed each other.

High priest. Like the mountains and rocks, may you protect each other.

High priestess. Like the Lady, may you be unending in your love and wisdom.

High priest. Like the Lord, may you be fierce in your love and passion.

High priest. Do you have tokens you wish to exchange at this time as symbols of your love and commitment to each other? *(Couples may exchange rings, amulets, or other sacred objects.)*

High priestess. Moonpiper, please repeat after me: "I, Moonpiper, give thee Windsong this token of my love for you. I promise to be sensitive to your needs. I will strive to give you space when you need it. I will strive to give you comfort when you need it. I will strive to give you encouragement when you need it. My love for you is honest. My love for you is passionate. My love for you is human. My love for you is divine. I will be your partner in creating a home and sacred sanctuary for us to share in our worship of the Lord and Lady. I will strive to give you love always."

High priest. Windsong, repeat after me: "I, Windsong, give thee Moonpiper this token of my love for you. I promise to be sensitive to your needs. I will strive to give you space when you need it. I will strive to give you comfort when you need it. I will strive to give you encouragement when you need it. My love for you is honest. My love for you is passionate. My love for you is human. My love for you is divine. I will be your partner in creating a home and sacred sanctuary for us to share in our worship of the Lord and Lady. I will strive to give you love always."

High priestess. Wherever Moonpiper and Windsong go, they go united, and they are united even when they are apart. May they rest always at home, even when physically separated. Let home be a sanctuary and a haven, a place for healing and growth.

High priest. Let home be a place of courage and integrity. Let fears be expressed honestly and promptly. Let anger be expressed healthily and not allowed to poison the relationship. Be strong in your love for yourselves and in your love for each other.

(At this point, if desired, the couple may perform the Great Rite or may jump over a broom. At this point also, a cord may be bound around the wrists of the couple as the officials speak.)

High priestess. Let this cord represent that you are united, two individuals with one common cause, one hope, one dream.

High priest. Let this cord represent that you enter into this partnership willingly, and that this knot is tied in accordance to your wishes.

High priestess. I pronounce you a wedded couple. You may kiss to seal your pledge.

High priest. We thank the elements of air, fire, water, and earth for their attendance this day and ask that the spirits of the elements go forth and herald this union. These two lives are now joined in one unbroken circle. We thank the Lord and Lady for blessing us with their divine presence.

High priestess. The circle is open but unbroken. Go in peace and love, taking the joy and celebration of this ceremony with you as you leave.

RUNES

......

BY DONALD TYSON

Runes are the symbolic tools of a system of magic created around 500 BCE by the shamans of warrior tribes living in the great forests of northern Europe. No one knows their origin. It is believed they resulted from a fusion between the native occult symbols of the shamans and the Etruscan and Latin alphabets.

Lured by the prospect of plunder, German mercenary clans crossed the Alps to fight in northern Italy. To the illiterate barbarians, written letters seemed magical. The shamans recognized a similarity between the letters used by the Etruscans and their own secret power symbols. Over generations, the shamans combined their own symbols with some of the Etruscan, and later Latin, letters and developed a system of writing to convey their native language.

Runes serve the balanced functions of letters for writing and symbols for ritual magic. Other alphabets, such as Hebrew and Enochian, are used for magical purposes, but they remain written letters with secondary magical associations. Each rune is equally a letter and a living power symbol for a force in nature.

These natural forces were, in early ages, humanized as gods and spirits. Most of the names of the gods have been forgotten. Today, only a handful of runes can be linked with specific gods. Even so, there is good reason to believe that each of the forces represented by individual runes was looked upon as a mighty spirit by the shamans. This is supported by the ancient division of the twenty-four German runes into three families (aettir) of eight runes.

Thus each rune is the sigil or seal of a deity, and may be used ritually to summon forth and command that deity for *human pourposes*. For example, the rune Teiwas ↑ is the symbol of the warrior god Tew, after whom Tuesday gets its name. Teutonic warriors cut this rune into their own flesh over their hearts to invoke Tew into their bodies just prior to battle. In this way they sought to become possessed by Tew, who was renowned for his courage and war skills.

The use of runes was not restricted to a particular group in society. Any man or woman might employ the runes for purposes such as protection against poison or to ease the pains of childbirth. However, ignorance carried a price. Each use of the runes involved a sacrifice to the rune gods, usually a sacrifice of blood. The gods were capricious and pitiless. If an insufficient payment was offered, they were thought to exact their own payment in kind. Rune spirits evoked to slay a foe might claim as their gift the life of someone beloved by the person who called them. It was generally considered prudent to leave runes to the shamans, who obtained the knowledge to use them through initiation.

After gashing himself upon the breast (and perhaps on the arms and legs) with rune symbols, the young shaman allowed himself to be tied to a wooden pillar or cross that represented the world tree. He remained suspended for nine days and nights without eating or drinking. At the climax of the rite, Woden possessed the initiate and passed on to him the knowledge of runes. Perhaps this appearance of Woden was pantomimed by the master shaman wearing a mask, who whispered the secret wisdom into the ear of his disciple.

We do not know whether women were formally initiated into the mysteries of the runes. However, we do know that there were female rune masters, renowned for their powers of scrying, healing, and cutting the runes for magical purposes. They enjoyed a position of authority in their tribes, but were regarded with a certain amount of dread by the people.

The purest set of runes that has survived to the present is the twenty-four symbol German futhark (a name that derives from the first six runes in the German rune alphabet: F, U, Th, A, R, K). Later rune alphabets, which evolved in Scandinavia, contain sixteen runes, and other alphabets that evolved in England contain twenty-eight (or thirty-three) runes. All these later rune sets were based upon the elder German futhark. For the purposes of ritual magic, this is the best rune alphabet to use, although Wiccans often prefer the English runes.

One ancient form of rune magic is divination. A branch was cut from a fruit-bearing tree, such as the apple, and divided into twenty-four short wands. The diviner carved a rune into each wand, then cast the wands onto a white cloth. Three wands were picked up in succession with the eyes directed heavenward, then interpreted.

All of the German runes can be made by simple vertical and diagonal strokes. They contain (in their purest, primal forms) no curved strokes and no horizontal strokes. This is a strong indication that they were designed to be incised into the thin green bark of a freshly cut wooden sapling across the grain. Each sapling could thus carry a written message, and it seems likely one early use of runes was to convey messages between the leaders of nomadic tribes.

Shamans carried runes in their heads, and inscribed the runes wherever their magic was required. The thing upon which the rune was cut became infused with the spirit and power of that rune. When runes were written on carved yew wands and other objects for magical purposes, they were grouped into significant sets of repetitions and could not be read as words. Groups of three and nine runes occur frequently, but the meaning of these sets is not understood.

The inscription of runes on large standing stones arose when the use of runes for magic began to give way to the use of runes as a decorative, formal way of writing. Runes were carved on stones to commemorate important events, to mark the boundaries of land, and to preserve the names of great people. These rune stones had no magical function.

Modern rune pebbles or tiles are without historical precedent. They descend from the old rural custom of selecting animal hides by lot. Personal symbols were marked upon flat pebbles, then one was drawn randomly from the group. Some of these personal symbols were runes, but there is no indication that the medieval farmers who employed them as emblems understood their meanings or magical uses.

The Elder Futhark

ᚠ	1 Fehu (Cattle)	ᚺ	9 Hagalaz (Hail)	↑	17 Teiwaz (War god)
ᚢ	2 Uruz (Aurochs)	ᚣ	10 Nauthiz (Need)	ᛒ	18 Berkana (Birch)
ᚦ	3 Thurisaz (Devil)	ᛁ	11 Isa (Ice)	ᛗ	19 Ehwaz (Horse)
ᚨ	4 Ansuz (God)	ᛃ	12 Jera (Year)	ᛗ	20 Mannaz (Man)
ᚱ	5 Raido (Riding)	ᛇ	13 Eihwaz (Yew)	ᛚ	21 Laguz (Water)
ᚲ	6 Kenaz (Torch)	ᛈ	14 Perth (Apple)	◇	22 Inguz (Fertility god)
ᚷ	7 Gebo (Gift)	ᛦ	15 Algiz (Defense)	ᛞ	23 Dagaz (Day)
ᚹ	8 Wunjo (Glory)	ᛋ	16 Sowelu (Sun)	ᛟ	24 Othila (Homeland)

Unusual Forms
of Divination

......

by Patricia Telesco

Alectromancy: observance of roosters eating grain

Axinomancy: scrutiny of a stone balanced on a red-hot axe

Cromniomancy: examination of growth in specially
planted onions

Felidomancy: divination by watching cat behavior and actions

Futomani: Shinto tradition of divining from shoulder blade
bone of a sacred deer

Gelomany: interpretation of hysterical laughter

Hippomancy: divination by watching the gait of
horses during ceremonial processions

Ichthyomancy: examinations of fish

Kin: Hittite form of divination, which is similar to contemporary Ouija boards; having a board, fields, and symbols with a moving object as a medium

Libanomancy: Babylonian divination by smoke from cedar shavings or specially prepared incense

Margaritomancy: inspecting actions of a charmed pearl in a covered pot

Md-Mo: Tibetan divination by white and black arrows

Myomancy: omens interpreted by sounds and actions of suddenly appearing mice

Oenomancy: forecasts by color, appearance, and taste of a wine

Omphalomancy: contemplation of one's navel

Phren-ba: Tibetan divination by rosary (mala) of 108 beads. Number of beads from random grasp fixes answer.

Podomancy: divination by foot soles

Sciomancy: prognostication by the size, shape, and changing appearance of shadows

Sycomancy: observations of drying fig leaves

Tyromancy: divination by cheese coagulation

Zoomancy: omens due to appearances of legendary beasts

Fun Things with the Tarot

......

by Silver RavenWolf

I understand you love working with your tarot deck, but you want to know if there is something more you can do with it? Of course there is!

Tell a story. Choose a card you are having difficulty with and make up a story. It can be any kind you pick. When you are finished, put the story and the card under your pillow before you go to sleep or put it on your altar. Not only will you understand the card better in the future, you may even hit upon a great tale to be told to friends later!

Pick a card, any card. This is great for family reunions, birthday parties, or New Year's Eve bashes. Fan the tarot deck and ask the first person to pick a card. This card will stand for the energies he or she will most need to stay in touch with during the year.

Use your tarot cards as props in spellcasting and ritual work. For example, if you are looking for abundance in your life, choose the Ace of Pentacles, Ten of Pentacles, and the Empress. Put them in the center of your altar, or on a table where they will not be disturbed. In a magic circle, burn a gold candle and meditate on bringing abundance toward yourself and your family.

Spend an evening developing your own tarot spreads. Not everyone accesses the astral in the same way, nor do they draw conclusions in the same manner. Design spreads that are specifically for your use. Perhaps there will be one you will use quite often. It may become your trademark!

Are your readings sometimes muddled? Have a divinatory tool nearby that is not the tarot. I suggest something like the Cartouche or rune cards so that the querent (the person you are reading for) can see the cards, too. If an area is cloudy, put down the other type of card on top of the tarot card to give you more insight.

Ever get one of those people who likes to play "Test the Card Reader?" You can stop this by asking their birthday before they come to see you. Utilize astrology or numerology to prepare for any querent. You don't have to be a crack astrologer to glean good information.

Hone your skills by working with numerous decks. Every deck has something new to share, a different way of perceiving an issue. Keep careful notes for yourself.

Use a double deck when reading. I read with a double deck for an entire summer. The results were most interesting. Double cards showed areas that needed to be stressed for the querent. To make things really interesting, mix two decks (they will have to be the same brand). Without looking, choose 72 cards. Do a few readings with them. Watch the interesting things that pop up.

Design your own deck of tarot cards. Blank decks can be purchased at New Age or metaphysical bookstores. Begin collecting pictures of what the various cards mean to you. You will be delighted with the outcome and it is a treasure to keep. In fact, you may find it such an enjoyable pastime that you design decks for friends using pictures they give you, plus things you find.

Make a game out of your cards. Design a board game or write a computer program. This is a great way to teach your children the meanings of cards. It can be as simple or as difficult as you wish.

THE ENOCHIAN
RITUAL OF JOHN DEE

······

BY DONALD TYSON

All that we know about Enochian magic is the result of a partnership between two men. For a period of seven years, from 1582 to 1589, the mathematician and scholar John Dee conducted a series of ritual séances with a paid crystal scryer, the alchemist Edward Kelley. The angels communicated with Dee through Kelley, a highly gifted spirit medium who was able to see and hear the angels with ease, not only within the depths of the crystal globe, but at times outside the stone as well. Dee's psychic ability was limited, only rarely did Dee see or hear the angels. This forced Dee to rely on Kelley for communication with the angels. This was a fortunate pairing, for it was with Dee that the angels sought to communicate—he was their chosen prophet.

The angels first contacted John Dee in his bedroom on the night of March 8, 1581, somewhere between ten and eleven o'clock, as Dee recorded in his diary:

It was the 8 day, being Wensday, hora noctis, 10, 11, the strange noyse in my chamber of knocking; and the voice, ten tymes repeated, somewhat like the shrich of an owle, but more longly drawn, and more softly, as it were in my chamber.

This interesting though inarticulate spiritual communication was repeated several times. Dee began to scry into a crystal ball in an effort to see and hear the spirits more clearly. Crystal scrying has an ancient and honorable history in England. The Druid Merlin was known to own a crystal globe in which he foresaw events. Crystal gazing was an accepted means for communicating with spirits along with other forms of scrying such as water divination and mirror divination. The idea was that spirits found it easier to appear if they had some sort of physical medium as a focus. The crystal acted as a little window into the realm of the spirits.

Dee did not record in his diary the ritual procedures he used during his own solitary attempted at crystal scrying. It was the custom to use ritual when scrying in the crystal, so we may assume that Dee employed a ritual structure, though it was probably quite simple. At a minimum it consisted of a prayer and invocation. Dee very probably prepared himself for the sessions by cleansing himself, and may have put on ritual articles of clothing or jewelry. Whatever procedure was used, it proved at least partially successful. He recorded in his diary:

May 25th, I had sight in [chrystallo] offered me, and I saw.

What he saw in the crystal was not recorded. Dee's successful attempts at scrying were infrequent. He realized he needed a scryer with a talent beyond his own if he was to achieve a fruitful communication with these spirits. He experimented with the psychic abilities of Barnabus Saul, a medium who at the time was having troubles with the law. On October 8, 1581, Saul gave Dee information concerning chests of books that had recently been discovered in Northhamptonshire, but Dee recorded Saul's vision: "I fownd no truth in it."

Dee reported in his diary that the next night while lying in bed in front of a fireplace, Saul "was strangely trubled by a spiritual creature abowt mydnight." The Enochian angels were willing to attempt to communicate through Saul, but found him to be an unsuitable instrument.

The attempts by the Enochian angels to reach Dee through Saul ceased at around the same time that Edward Kelley arrived at Dee's house in Mortlake. On March 6, 1582, Saul came to visit. Dee recorded in his diary: "He confessed that he neyther hard or saw any spiritual creature any more." Two days later, Edward Kelley, traveling under the false name Talbot, arrived at Dee's home along with a mutual friend named Clerkson. Saul left Mortlake that same day, at around two or three o'clock in the afternoon, presumably after Kelley's arrival. It would be interesting to learn what took place between Saul and Kelley when they confronted each other.

It was on the night of March 8, the same day Kelley arrived at Mortlake, that one of the Enochian angels first visited him.

It probably appeared to Kelley while he was lying in bed. Kelley was able to see and hear the angel clearly enough to learn from it all about the deceit of Saul.

The first contact of the Enochian angels with John Dee occurred exactly one year to the day prior to Edward Kelley's arrival at Mortlake. Kelley came to Mortlake to discuss with Dee an alchemical manuscript in Kelley's possession called the Book of Dunstan, which the alchemist believed to contain the secret of the red powder. Dee was renowned throughout Europe as a scholar of recondite subjects. However, given the coincidence of dates, I cannot believe that Kelley's arrival was mere chance. I believe the Enochian angels somehow contrived to initiate his journey to Mortlake in order to bring Dee and Kelley together.

No matter the circumstances, it was immediately obvious to Dee that Kelley was the perfect scryer to communicate with the spiritual beings who had for the past year been trying to reach him. Kelley first scryed into the crystal two days after his arrival at Mortlake, on March 10, 1582. The crystal was an egg-shaped globe of polished but cloudy quartz, set in a frame that took the form of a vertical band of gold with four supporting legs and a cross on its top. The scrying session occurred in Dee's study, probably late in the afternoon. The time of day can be inferred since the angel Annael appeared to Saul on December 21, 1581, and told him to scry with the crystal bathed in the sunlight from the western window in Dee's study.

Kelley followed this procedure. He placed the crystal in its frame on the outer corner of Dee's writing desk, in a beam of sunlight. Dee sat down behind the desk to record in a diary Kelley's observation and all that the Enochian angels might say to Kelley. Thanks to Dee's rigorous adherence to this practice, the Enochian conversations have the accuracy of legal transcripts. Kelley did not sit, but knelt on the floor in front of Dee's desk. Kelley began to pray and invoked aloud the angel Annael into the stone. When this did not bring immediate success, Dee arose and went into his oratory, a small room attached to his study, to pray. Within fifteen minutes, Kelley reported seeing an angel in the depths of the stone. This angel revealed itself as Uriel and immediately began to transmit part of the Enochian system of magic.

In the following months, Dee and Kelley communicated regularly with the angels. Apart from the extemporaneous prayers that Dee recited to open and close the ritual, there was little outward formality. Dee did always maintain an attitude of reverential awe when communicating with the angels, as he was convinced throughout that they were the true angels of God. Kelley could never convert Dee to his own opinion that the Enochian angels were liars and deceivers.

Through Kelley, the angels transmitted instructors for the construction of ritual furniture and instruments. These were designed to make communications with the angels more certain. The chief of these was the elaborately inscribed "Table of Practice," a wooden table with four legs that was painted in various colors, with Enochian letters on its top. Its overall shape was cubic; thirty-six inches on each side. Dee finished it on April 29, 1582. Upon it were set (or perhaps painted) seven elaborate seals called the "Ensigns of Creation," arranged in a large circle. The Ensigns corresponded to the spheres of the seven planets of traditional astrology. Within the circle of the Ensigns was the most important of the ritual instruments, the "Sigillum Aemeth" (Seal of Truth), a wax seal nine inches in diameter.

The Sigillum Aemeth is the power object of Enochian magic. It was inscribed with a detailed and beautiful design in the form of a pentagram set within a heptagon set within two interlocking heptagrams set within a larger heptagon. All of these shapes were surrounded by a great circle of forty segments. The names of several Enochian spirits appear on the seal, as well as individual letters and numbers. At its very center is the name Levanael, a spirit of the moon. Enochian magic is lunar magic. Monday, the day of the moon, was the day chosen by the angels for the most important scrying sessions. The entire elaborate structure of Enochian magic is based on the number seven and on the seven planetary spheres in a cycle beginning with the moon and Monday.

The scrying crystal was laid upon a small cushion on top of the Sigillum Aemeth, which acted as the key to open the crystal and allow the true Enochian angels to appear within its depths. This was not the same crystal that had been used by Barnabas Saul, but a new crystal that miraculously appeared on the floor of Dee's study on April 28, 1582. While scrying in the old crystal on that day, Kelley happened to look toward the western window and noticed a gleaming object on the floor. He had a vision in which a small angel with a flaming sword in hand picked up the object and extended it toward Dee. The angel Michael told Dee through Kelley, "Go toward it and take it up." So Dee approached the window. At first he saw nothing, but then he noticed something on the floor. It was the crystal that would become his "principal stone."

It is quite likely that Kelley placed this crystal on the floor. But in my opinion, he was possessed by one of the Enochian angels while doing so and retained no knowledge of his actions. Dee simply accepted the appearance of the stone as miraculous.

It became a part of the ritual furniture, along with the Table, Ensigns, Sigillum Aemeth, and other ritual instruments such as a magic seal ring and a lamen, both designed to be worn by Dee during the Enochian rituals.

The principal showstone was placed on its cushion on top of the wax Sigillum Aemeth in the center of the Table of Practice, surrounded by the seven Ensigns. The Ensigns were not visible but hidden beneath a cloth. Candles were lit to cast light on either side of the stone. A red silk carpet lay on the floor under the table. Kelley sat at the table and scryed into the stone while Dee recorded the sayings and doings of the angels. Prayers were used to open and close the ritual. Dee probably wore the seal ring and the lamen. There is no mention in the Enochian transcripts of casting a magical circle around the table, but one may have been used. Kelley was a necromancer and would have been familiar with magic circles.

Many details were left unrecorded by Dee. It is impossible to reconstruct the ritual precisely. On the other hand, we are fortunate that the records kept by Dee over a period of seven years have preserved so much of Enochian magic. We at least know the instruments constructed by Dee under the direction of the angels. Without Dee's transcript of the conversations with the angels, neither Enochian magic nor the Enochian language would even exist today.

THE ORISHAS OF SANTERÍA

······

BY MARGUERITE ELSBETH

Orishas are the African deities of Santeria, a rich and vibrate nature religion based on stones, seashells, water, and herbs. The Yoruba slaves who brought the religion from Africa identified the orishas with the Catholic saints in order to preserve the tradition. Therefore, practicing santeros, or priests, recognize the saints as having the same supernatural powers as the orishas for healing and spellcasting.

As the practitioners of Santeria believe in one creative force, called Oloddumare, the orishas are worshiped as spirit guardians who offer divine guidance and protection to reverent followers, rather than as gods. Every individual in the Santeria religion has a personal orisha to help him or her along the path of life.

Eleggua *(St. Anthony)* is a trickster, tending to create confusion wherever he goes. Because he knows all things, he demands his due before all other deities. Eleggua brings us into balance and wholeness.

Orunmila *(St. Francis of Assisi)* is "one who lives both in heaven and earth." Divination is his gift to humankind. Because he knows our ultimate fate, he helps us to improve our destiny.

Obatala *(Our Lady of Mercy)* is a male deity, embodying female aspects also. He is known for peace, purity, and the white robes in which he dresses. Obatala helps us to control our thoughts.

Chango *(St. Barbara)* is the patron of power. He wears a red coat covered with cowrie shells and is fond of women, food, dancing, thunder, lightning—all things hot and fiery. He can help us to attain passion in our relationships.

Oggun *(St. Peter)* is a warrior god, and the patron of all metals. Although he creates as much chaos here on Earth, he also helps us gain employment and protects us against violent crime.

Ochosi *(St. Norbert)* is the divine hunter. He resides in the woods, sometimes "eating and living" with Oggun. Ochosi protects and assists hunters. He also has curative powers, and can help with relocation, as well as courtroom trials.

Aganyu *(St. Christopher)* is the volcano god, and the father of Chango through his union with Yemmu. One can only receive Aganyu's helpful control over harmful influences through Chango's intercession.

Babalu-Aye *(St. Lazarus)* is the patron of healing, and one of the most respected and well-loved orishas. He carries a bag filled with corn, and he helps those in financial distress achieve prosperity.

Yemaya *(Our Lady of Regla)* is an ocean goddess and a patroness of fertility. This much-revered orisha is very beautiful. She brings young girls to womanhood and is associated with the moon.

Oshun *(Our Lady of Charity)* is a river goddess, the Venus-Aphrodite of the Santeria religion. She is the patroness of love, marriage, money, joy, and abundance.

Oya *(Our Lady of Candelaria/St. Teresa)* is the goddess of the winds and the cemeteries. Because she is a warrior, her behavior is very aggressive. She offers her followers protection against death.

References

Santeria: The Religion by Migene Gonzalez-Wippler.

WITCH BALLS

······

BY AMBER K

Folklore gives us many ways to protect and bless our homes, from a sprig of rowan fastened near the entryway to the brightly colored hex signs of the Pennsylvania Dutch to the inverted horse shoe nailed above the door to "catch the luck" and hold it. The witch ball is one more protective device.

A witch ball is a hollow glass sphere hung at a window, near the hearth, or in a corner of the room near the ceiling that averts or traps evil before it can bring harm to the occupants of the home. It may be only a couple of inches in diameter, or large as a pumpkin.

Some writers have said they were called witch balls because they were made to protect a home from witches. It is just as possible, however, that the balls were used by witches to ward their own homes, and those of their clients.

No one knows exactly when these talismans first were used. The manufacture of glass and the ability to make blown-glass vessels are very old skills; the Roman Empire had a lovely trade in glass two thousand years ago. We know that witch balls were common in colonial America.

Many witch balls were coated inside with silver nitrate. It was said that these reflected the evil eye or any negative spell back on the sender. Also, any demon seeing his face reflected in the silver ball would be frightened and flee, or maybe seeing the world reflected in a curved, distorted way was enough to confuse him. Other balls are created with slender threads or pillars of glass inside to catch any evil spirit that ventured within. Yet others were simply the glass balls, clear or green or blue, used by fishermen to float their nets. Perhaps they were reflective enough to work in the same way as the silver balls.

Witch balls have also found their way into the garden in the form of the large gazing globes on pedestals that adorned many Victorian gardens and are still seen occasionally today. If a flower garden is a place of beauty and serenity, a refuge from the cares of the world, certainly it deserves protection as much as the house itself.

Another place where witch balls turn up is on the family Christmas tree—or more accurately the Yule tree, as the custom of dragging a tree indoors is doubtlessly Pagan in origin. The tree may be a variant on the Yule log, which was originally a huge dead tree (and phallic symbol), conveyed to the manor house by the men of the village with much singing and ribald horseplay. There one end was placed in the great hearth and a fire kindled. Over several days of feasting and festivity the Yule log was gradually pushed into the fire as the end was consumed.

The Yule tree may also have been a representation of the world tree of old northern Europe. The whole universe was imagined as a great ash tree, called Yggdrasil. Its roots reached down into the Norse underworlds, Niflheim and Muspelheim; its crown stretched up to Asgard and the halls of the gods; and in its branches deer and other wild creatures browsed. This great tree is akin to the tree of life of the ancient goddess civilizations of the near East.

On our Yule trees today we place lights and stars and candy canes, carved animals and elves and Santas and—of course— little glass spheres. Witch balls. Gold for the reborn sun god and silver for the moon goddess, whose blessings and protection we ask for the coming new year. In *Ancient Ways* (Llewellyn, 1991), Pauline Campanelli suggests that the "shiny glass balls catch the light of the newborn sun and send it back as a magical means of enhancing the sun's energy."

You can have your own witch ball up year round. Buy a large and beautiful Yule ornament or seek out a glass fisherman's float in an antique shop, or look in a catalog of garden statuaries for a gazing globe. Give it a special place of honor in your home or garden, invoke the gods of your choice, and consecrate it to its protective purpose. Dust it frequently to remove any negativity from its surface. Perhaps it will make your home that much more of a safe haven.

Banishing

······

by Elizabeth Genco

Some years ago when I first began exploring Wicca on my own, I struggled (as most of us do) to make sense of the myriad conflicting practices. Magical and ritual work had the most complications to sort out. Instructions in books would contradict each other, or I would get bogged down in the "how to" or in lists of obscure ingredients (where does one find mandrake and lodestones, anyway?), second-guessing myself every step of the way. It's a common problem, borne of a religion in which there are many paths to the same destination. Despite the fact that there was much that I didn't understand about magic, a few things came easily—almost instinctively. These intuitive workings included a series of powerful banishings, performed when I was an absolute beginner (more or less).

Sound odd? I suppose it was. After all, "banishing" is one of those loaded words that (pardon the pun) conjures up images of old hags at the crossroads, burying foul remnants of sympathetic magic, muttering curses at the poor fool who made the unfortunate misstep of crossing her. There is as much archetypal baggage associated with the act of banishing as there is, well, with the word "witch." To many, "banishing" and "witch" are inextricably linked, and intrinsically negative.

So what business did I have mucking around with banishing back then? Indeed, what is a modern magical practitioner to do with it now?

Like all magic, the key to banishing lies in its purpose and the object of the working, which brings us directly to ethics. A discussion of Wicca's main ethical tenet, "harm none," is outside of the scope of this article; ultimately, each practitioner will have to come to grips with its implications, and the line of what constitutes "harm" will be different for each. When I did accept formal training, it was with a group that explicitly prohibits workings that interfere with the free will of another; in fact, my tradition puts its money where its mouth is and requires an oath to that effect. Among the Wiccans I know, "harm none" is serious business, and a banishing that impedes with another's free will in any way is out of the question.

Fortunately, my use of banishing doesn't conflict with my oaths, and never did. Though it has always had a reputation as manipulative magic, and, indeed, can be put to ill use, baneful banishing is only a small part of the story (you know, like the images of green-faced hags passed off as witches in the popular consciousness). My banishings, then and now, are designed to help me deal with those things inside myself that hinder my personal growth. Such workings are moving, cathartic experiences. A personally designed, carefully crafted banishing can be one of the most affirming tools in a modern witch's toolbox.

At its most basic level, "banishing" is simply another word for a cleansing. A ritual clearing of magical space or objects before a rite could be called a banishing, as could a clearing of a dwelling after a negative event. When used for personal growth, a banishing is a cleansing of the self, designed to sever ties with those things within us that no longer serve us. The implications of the magic are powerful: by clearing our internal garden, we make room for something new and better to take root and grow.

What sorts of internal baggage might you want to banish? Maybe you've been plagued by a bad habit for years, such as smoking, drinking, or overeating; a banishing can help you begin or continue your road to recovery. Maybe you've just gone through some kind of personal upheaval, such as a layoff or an eviction, and have been left with lingering feelings of self-doubt and disempowerment; a banishing can help you work through these emotions and move on. If it's really necessary, a banishing can help you put an end to something inconsequential but still annoying, such as biting your nails or saying "y'know?" too many times in one day. Personally, I have used banishing to get rid of self-doubts and put an end to the negative chattering voices in my head. Just about anything can be adopted to a personal-growth banishing, as long as it is about you. The focus on you is important, not only because of the ethical and karmic issues, but because personal magic is the most effective.

Once you've pinpointed a problem and have decided to take action, you might be tempted to skip straight to a working. Resist that urge. Take some time to meditate on exactly what you are banishing and why. By performing a banishing, you relinquish a part of yourself forever. It's a big step, and thus merits extra consideration. You might wish to enlist the aid of a divinatory tool, too. Here are some questions to ask yourself before performing a banishing:

What, exactly, do I wish to banish? Clearly articulating what you wish to be rid of will establish important boundaries.

Why do I wish to banish this? There should be a clear motive behind your working.

What purpose has it served in my life up to now? All of our behaviors serve a certain purpose—even so-called bad behaviors. What purpose does the behavior in question serve now? The behavior you wish to banish may indeed be draining you, but by asking this question, you are making sure that it does not still help you in some way. And even though you will be asking a part of yourself to move on, it is still a part of you, and its contributions to your well-being should be acknowledged.

How is what I wish to banish preventing me from moving forward? The flip side to the previous question.

What do I hope to gain from this banishing?

Am I prepared to deal with any unforeseen consequences of this banishing? All magic sets into motion forces that we cannot stop. Once the cork is out of the bottle, so to speak, we are no longer fully in control. You won't be able to foresee all possible outcomes of your working. Considering ahead of time what results other than what you intended that might arise is also helpful.

Though personal-growth banishing is a positive step, it is permanent, and not to be taken lightly. Be sure that it's what you really need to do.

Some magical practitioners will tell you that magic should be performed, then "forgotten;" that is to say, out of one's mind so that the work can take hold. Certain kinds of banishing, however, should be backed up with action in the mundane world. For example, it would be unrealistic to expect to stop smoking without a concentrated, regular conscious effort. In cases where you're fighting some serious demons, consider creating an action plan consisting of magical and mundane steps designed to maximize your success.

Petition Magic

Petition work is among my favorite flavors of magic. Its effectiveness comes from its simplicity; namely, it relies on the power of the written word to give tangible form to that which you want to eliminate, and then the cleansing energy of fire to clear it away.

Simple Banishing

This spell can be used for something small, or if you're just getting used to the idea of banishing. It can be used for "the big stuff," too, and can be repeated as needed.

You'll need a slip of clean white paper, a pen (I prefer black ink but use whatever color suits), tweezers, a lighter or lit candle, a small cauldron or some other fireproof dish, and sea salt.

To prepare, gather all of your materials at your altar or chosen working area. Place a little sea salt in the bottom of the cauldron. The salt will create an uneven surface, which will allow for the flow of oxygen around the paper and will result in a better flame.

Create sacred space in whatever way you'd like. When you're ready, take the pen and write what you'd like to banish on the slip of paper. Fold the paper and hold it with the tweezers. With an image of what you're banishing firmly in your mind, light the paper.

As the paper burns down, imagine yourself free of whatever you banish. As the flame engulfs the paper, drop it into the cauldron.

After your ritual, scatter the ashes outside or flush them down the toilet, continuing your visualization.

Witch Bottle Spell

This spell is a bit more involved, and can be used for more than one banishment at a time, or to go deeper with a particular banishment. It evokes some of the old stereotypes of witches and banishing, but turns them on their head to create a positive, personal experience.

You'll need a small glass bottle (with cork, stopper, or some other means of closure), a candle in the appropriate color (your choice), slips of white paper, and a pen. You can also include other small objects relating to your banishment if you wish.

Gather your materials and create sacred space in your usual manner. When you're ready, begin to write what you want to banish on the slip(s) of paper. If your intention is made of a few different parts, or you wish to banish more than one thing, write each one on a separate slip of paper. As you finish writing down each banishment, drop each slip into the bottle. Visualize that part of you falling into the bottle along with the paper. If you have other objects relating to your banishment, add those now.

When you have finished, top the bottle with its cork or stopper. Light the candle and drip wax over the top of the bottle to seal.

Next, dispose of the bottle in some manner you feel is appropriate. Burying the bottle works well, as does tossing it in a large body of water. These aren't my favorite methods, however, since they aren't environmentally friendly. We live in a modern age; as such, I prefer a ceremonial disposal in the trash!

As you dispose of the bottle, visualize your banishments breaking away from you. Bid them a gentle, thankful farewell, for they have served a certain purpose in your life, and, until now, you needed them in some way. Send them on with light and love.

Ritual Housecleaning

Sometimes we have distinct physical manifestations of what we're trying to get rid of in our home or other environments. Clean house with this simple but effective procedure. (This one is particularly good for dieters—you can get rid of all those unhealthy snacks in the kitchen!)

Going from room to room, gather up any and all objects that you'd like to get rid of that pertain to your banishment intention. When you have them all, bring them to your working area and create sacred space.

Visualize what you'd like to banish gently falling away from you. Acknowledge that the objects before you are physical representations of parts of you that served you well at one point in your life, but are no longer needed. Give thanks for what these banishments have given you in the past, then state your intention to move on. Take as much time as you need, then close your ritual. Dispose of all objects gathered immediately.

MESSAGE IN A BOTTLE: THE HISTORY OF THE WITCH BOTTLE

......

BY SALLY MCSWEENEY

Imagine that you have decided to do some work on the front porch of the eighteenth-century house into which you have just moved. As construction of the foundation proceeds, a worker notices the glint of sunlight on something green, half buried in the earth. Carefully they loosen the soil around it and pull forth a small green bottle that, when opened, reveals small pieces of metal, a nail, and a piece of dark leather. This is exactly what happened in 2005 in Lincolnshire, England. Archaeological research showed that it was a witch bottle dating to the early 1800s, which is quite late for such a bottle to have been made.

A large number have been found dating back to at least the early 1600s in England; the first found in the United States was on Tinicum Island in the Delaware River south of Philadelphia in 1976. This dated back to the mid-1700s and contained six pins, a piece of bird bone, and a pottery shard.

Despite the use of the word "bottle," which we tend to associate with glass, they were more often made of stoneware glazed with salt. These originated in Germany in the sixteenth century and were called "bartmanns" or "bellarmines." The name comes from a man called Cardinal Bellarmine, a Catholic inquisitor, and they carried a picture resembling him that showed a very stern-looking image. Glass was not generally used in England until later centuries. From where we stand today, the early bottles were certainly not made following the recent popular maxim of "harm none." Such a bottle was originally created by a "victim" for counter-sorcery—to banish evil or negative magic directed at them, particularly from a suspected witch who was thought to have sent a curse. Its contents were used not just to simply repel this energy, but also to actually cause suffering to the witch. The bottles were filled with objects such as broken pottery or glass, bent rusty nails, pins, thorns, and small pieces of bone. Sometimes the victim added some of their hair or nail clippings—and even urine or blood.

There are a couple of theories behind the use of urine in the bottles. It was believed that the witch had created a magical and psychic bond between herself and her chosen recipient that could be reversed and/or broken by the making of the bottle. The curse acted most strongly upon the bodily fluids of the victim, so by putting some of her urine in the spell bottle, the curse fell upon this first before it reached the actual person. In this way, the curse was dissolved. Secondly, the urine was thought to hold "part of the vital spirit of the witch" as a result of the working of her curse through the link. When the witch next went to pass water, she would supposedly feel all sorts of torment—sharp pain sent by the sympathetic magic of the nails or pins. In this way, the curse was sent back to her. Strong stuff indeed! The bottle was buried in a place where it would not be disturbed, often under the hearth where the heat from the fire was thought to activate the metal objects within the urine, resulting in the breaking of the curse. The hearth was also a logical place for a witch bottle because it was believed that witches entered houses through the chimney. The bottles have also been found in attics and inside walls. The magic of the bottle remained active for as long as the bottle was hidden and unbroken.

Hopefully today, you won't need to be making a witch bottle for quite such a grim purpose, but they can be used for a variety of magical reasons and placed in various chosen spots; like all magical tools they are a focal point for your energy and intent. They are most commonly made to capture negative energies without harming the sender. Craft stores and thrift stores are great resources for bottles; there is a plethora available to choose from, but do make sure that it has a tight stopper or lid. You can use glass, earthenware, or stoneware bottles. The items you wish to place in it will determine the size. Most spell bottles are made on the night of the full moon, but for those of a banishing nature, the dark moon phase is appropriate. Be careful when constructing your bottle, as some of the objects will be sharp.

A witch bottle can be a powerful means to protect your home or property; bury one at each corner of your land and/or by the front door. If you live in an apartment, bury it in a plant pot by the door. To make such a bottle, you will need some dried rosemary, three pinches of salt, nine pins, three metal nails, and red wine. (You may replace the red wine with urine and/or menstrual blood if you want to stay true to tradition.) Place all the items in the bottle and say:

Herb of protection, blood red wine,
Pins and nails, guard me and mine.

To protect a particular person, place a picture of the person in the jar and surround it with sharp objects such as broken glass, pins or needles, nails, and thorns. The intent is to build a "wall" around the person that will keep any harm at bay. To capture negativity, fill a bottle with similar objects and tangled thread that will ensnare the hostility and prevent it from reaching you. Bury the bottle away from the home where it is unlikely to be found; an ideal place would be a swamp or a bog.

To protect against psychic attack, you will need to break a small mirror, which under these circumstances, will not bring bad luck. Put the pieces in your bottle with nine nails. Light a black candle and say:

Candle lit, burning low
Stop attacks, here and now.
Broken mirror to reflect
Any harm that comes to wreck.
Nails of steel, nine be true
Allow no evil to get through.

Variations
To make a love bottle, try to find a red glass bottle. You will need some dried rose petals, three pinches of dried lavender, three

drops of rose oil, a nine-inch piece of red ribbon, a coin, and some red wine. Tie two knots in the ribbon and tie the ends together. This symbolizes the joining of you and a partner. Place the ribbon, rose, lavender, and the coin into the bottle. The coin represents the investment you are going to make in finding the right person for you. Add the rose oil; with each successive drop say "my heart, your heart, our hearts." Fill the bottle with the red wine and imagine your life filling with love as you pour. Put the lid on the bottle where it will be undisturbed. In the event that the relationship with the person who comes into your life does not work out or you wish to end the relationship, open the bottle, pour out the wine, and cut the ribbon between the knots. Bury all the contents.

A popular witch bottle today is an abundance or money bottle. For this you will need one made of green glass. You will also need a silver coin, three pinches of cinnamon, three pinches of basil, three corn kernels, and a piece of citrine. If you have a small pentacle add this; if not, draw one on some paper. The pentacle represents wealth in the tarot. Put the items into the bottle and say:

Sparkling silver, shiny and round,
Into my life, may money be bound.
Herbs of abundance, stone and grain,
Work your magic so money I'll gain.

Then, using a green candle, seal the lid.

My personal favorite is a psychic power bottle, which can be made in a couple of ways. It should be put together on the night of the new moon and be left where it can (hopefully) bathe in the waxing moonlight until the full moon. I have a wonderful engraved, silver brandy flask that dates from 1810, which is perfect because silver is the metal most associated with the moon. You can use it for astral travel, divination enhancement, dream work or ritual, and for these purposes you will need to put nine pinches of mugwort in your bottle and then add some virgin olive oil. Anoint yourself with a little of the oil whenever you want to enhance your psychic abilities. As mugwort is considered the most potent herb for divination work, it is also used to cleanse crystals, amulets, crystal balls, and so on. For this purpose, add spring water instead of oil to the mugwort in your bottle and use this to "bathe" your object in. For both bottles say:

Within the darkness of the night,
By growing light of magical moon,
And from the herb of second sight,
To me will come this power soon.

As you kneel in the soft earth of the flowerbed beside your front door, the silver light of the full moon casts its magical illumination upon the small hole you have dug there. Gently, you place your silver witches bottle in the hole; before you cover it with the moist soil, you catch a glimpse of your face reflected in the shiny surface. But was it your face? It looked different somehow. Patting the soil down, you smile as you feel the connection with countless women who have done such magic before you and you wonder if, in years to come, another such woman will find your hidden treasure.

TANTRIC DREAM YOGA

······

BY KENNETH JOHNSON

When most people hear the word tantra, they think of "sexual yoga." Although this is an important part of the tantric tradition, it's not the whole story. Tantra is the "magic" of India, and includes ritual, mantra, talismanic magic, and a whole universe of goddess mythology in additional to the sexual techniques. By way of example, here is a dream yoga from the tantric tradition designed to help you access the goddess or god who will appear to you as your inner dream lover.

Begin by making sure that your sleep will be as restful as possible. Make your final meal of the day a light one, and get some mild exercise before bed. Best of all, release your daily anxieties through reading, listening to peaceful music, or meditating. Try to sleep in a clean, quiet, well-ventilated room decorated in soft blues or greens.

Lie down on your back with your hands folded over your solar plexus. If you still feel too restless to fall asleep, visualize a blue flame burning at the base of your spine between your genitals and your anus—the psychic center or chakra that is called the *muladhara* or root chakra in Hindu occultism. Allow the light of the blue flame to spread out in all directions through your body. When at last you are perfectly restful and calm, affirm that your dreams will contact the higher powers whose guidance you seek. Then silently repeat the words "dream lover, dream lover, come to me now." Do this several times.

Try to fall asleep lying on your right side with your knees slightly bent, the left leg on top of the right one, and the right cheek cupped in your right hand. Your left arm will lie on your left leg. Traditionally, you should be facing north, although this isn't absolutely necessary.

When you wake up, record your dreams before doing anything else. If you remember only vague fragments, then record the fragment. If you remember absolutely nothing, record the first thought that was in your mind when you woke up. If you wake up during the night, record whatever you may remember from the dream state, though in general, the most important dreams will be those that occur just before waking in the morning.

After a week or so, examine your dream journal, paying special attention to dreams that take place in another time period or in unusual surrounding as well as meetings, conversations, or activities invoking people whom you do not know in ordinary life. Pay special attention to sexual symbolism. Be creative. Sexual symbolism is everywhere, if you know where to look for it. Don't be afraid of being naughty or feeling like a Freudian.

In time the sexual symbols will constellate around a relationship with a particular dream character. Hindus and Tantric Buddhists regard such a dream lover as a goddess or god, one of the divine sexual beings called *dakas* (if masculine) or *dakinis* (if feminine). As a Westerner, you are more likely to meet your dream lover in the form of a movie star, casual stranger, the boy or girl next door, or some mysterious, unknown personage.

When you finally meet your dream lover, the process leaps to a whole new level. Every time you encounter him or her during sleep, you must remember to meditate on the dream as soon as you wake up. Recreate the entire dream in your mind. As you replay the dream, examine its content and its symbols with as much conscious awareness and detachment as you can muster.

Repeated contemplation of the important dreams wherein you meet your dream lover will in time lead you to yet another level. According to tantric tradition, your meditations will eventually guide you out of yourself, traveling along the silver cord that attaches your astral body to your physical body. You will be guided into a whole new universe. There, in that other reality, you will come face-to-face with the magical being who has brought you this far, and who has chosen to act as your initiator and spirit guide in the other world.

BELLY DANCING, THE RITE
THAT HONORS THE GODDESS

......

BY EMELY FLAK

On a warm, sultry evening somewhere in a busy metropolitan hub, someone plays some music with a Middle Eastern beat. Women dance to the music to celebrate their collective femininity and individual shape. Bare bellies shimmy, bare feet rustle across the polished wooden floor; the women take pride in their varied appearance. All of them are beautiful and resplendent in a rainbow of floating chiffon interspersed with noisy gold and silver accessories.

Such is a belly dancing class in an Australian adult learning center, the latest craze across many industrialized Western countries. In such classes, women of all sorts gather to dance and so rejoice together and reconnect to ancient goddess energies.

History of Belly Dancing

Although difficult to pinpoint its beginnings, belly dancing evolved from ancient spiritual movements that honored fertility. As the survival of our species relied on our success in reproducing, our ancestors devised rituals such as the belly dance to gain favors from the fertility goddess. The earthy, sensual movements are said to unite the body with the spirit of the earth. This dance evolved into what the French named *danse due ventre*, or "dance of the belly," which was first demonstrated in the United States at the Chicago World's Fair in 1896 by a dancer identified only as Little Egypt. The Americans translated its French name into "belly dancing." We now associate the belly dance with Middle Eastern tradition.

This dance form has been labeled as obscene and primitive due to its subtle and not so subtle sexual overtones. Despite efforts over the age to eradicate this body-centered, exotic dance form, the belly dance has survived to enjoy a revival with many contemporary Western women.

So what is it about the dance that has attracted a high level of interest? Multicultural influences in Western society have enabled us to experience a diversity of food, languages, and customs. In turn, this has made us more culturally sensitive and less judgmental. It is quite common for diners to be entertained by a belly dancer on a busy night in most Middle Eastern restaurants. Meanwhile, growing interest in the dance has also been linked to the increased independence of women. Belly dancing can be seen as an empowering activity for women.

Details of Belly Dancing

Belly dancing is designed specifically for the shape of the female body. The hips undulate in isolation from the rest of the
body in a circular motion. The circle, a symbol of protection,
represents the Great Mother Goddess in a tribal context. The
hips move in the shape of the figure eight, making the movements hypnotic. Kinesiologists have recognized that figure-eight
body movements that cross the center line of the body activate
neurons connecting the left and right brain hemispheres. The
dancer also isolates upper body movements, alternating with vibrating shimmy movements. Combined with the fluid actions
carried out by the arms, belly dancing engages all parts of the
body, including an internal massage of the reproductive and di-
gestive organs. Belly dancing involves low-impact exercise, and
it strengthens back muscles. Belly dancing is a healthy physical
workout that suits women at all stages of their life. Furthermore,
by dancing barefoot, the belly dancer connects with the Great
Mother Goddess, with the earth, and with nature.

This dance form has evolved over thousands of years and
varies a great deal in the use of accessories. The props used, like
swords, veils, candles, and even snakes, have magical and primitive roots. Some dancers use finger zills, adding interest, color,
and sound to the performance. Dancers apply their individual-
ity and freedom of expression through their choice of accessories
and their costume.

Even today, some traditions continue to recognize the fertility
element of this dance. At an Egyptian wedding, the bride and
groom often engage the services of a belly dancer. The couple
places their hands on the dancer's stomach to ensure their own

bounty. Interestingly, the fertility aspect of belly dancing has also emerged as a useful exercise for childbirth. Fernand Lamaze, in his childbirth classes, recommended pelvic rocking movements, similar to those in belly dancing, to shorten the duration of labor and to ease the pain of giving birth.

In a culture where slim, emaciated bodies are promoted as the paragon of feminine beauty, belly dancing is an art form that reveres the curvy female contour. Abundance in flesh is considered a bonus and belly dancers of all sizes and ages discover and enjoy confidence in displaying their shape. Women dancing together create an atmosphere of empowerment and trust. Now studied and practiced as an art form, many belly dancers in Middle Eastern restaurants, cabarets, and functions are women who have discovered a passion in keeping this ancient dance ritual alive.

CEREMONIAL MAGIC AND
THE AVERAGE PERSON

......

BY ESTELLE DANIELS

When they get into magic, many people come into contact with the magical system known as ceremonial magic. Perhaps it is cloaked in other guises, like Enochian, thelema, kabbalah, thaumaturgy, or geomancy, but it's out there and quite widespread. Much of ceremonial magic is quite formula oriented. It demands a thorough knowledge of astrology, kabbalah, and other disciplines, and knowledge of Hebrew would be very useful also. This is more than the average person is willing to take on just to see if that system is right for them.

There are, however, a couple of rituals used in ceremonial magic that are easily done and very accessible to all. The lesser banishing ritual of the pentagram (LBPR for short) and the rose cross are fairly simple and work well with most any tradition or style. They can be used by themselves, together, or be adapted to work with other types of circles and magical techniques. In our classes we make the students learn and memorize these rituals so they are available to them at all times. The reason is that they are simple, effective, and when done correctly, they always produce results. No matter what state of mind you are in, no matter where you are, if you say the correct words and go through the motions, these rituals will produce a result. And if you put energy into them and add the proper visualizations, the results are more effective.

This is because since these rituals were developed they have been in continuous use by magicians. This has built up a cosmic energy bank on the astral, so that anyone who uses them can tap into that vast magical reservoir and benefit thereby. These rituals are also ones that cannot cause harm if done incorrectly. In other words, if you accidentally say the wrong word or visualize an incorrect color, you will not blow up, get an energy backlash, or be harmed. The worst that can happen is that nothing will happen. This is important because people can be apprehensive if they have heard some of the legends and folklore built up around ceremonial magic.

These two rituals are both magical circles. They create a sacred space that is cleansed and consecrated and can also provide a measure of insulation and protection to those within the circle. They are also automatic circles, and dissipate on their own. They do not need to be taken down. They are quite good for divination. Divination within a circle is more effective, for you are screening out all the everyday static and noise. You can concentrate better and can tap into the fountains of inspiration more easily.

Ceremonial magic is quite old, though it has been growing, changing, and evolving since ancient times. Most of the ceremonial magical rituals and spells are based upon kabbalah and hermeticism, with liberal doses of other occult disciplines thrown in. These can be argued to be the descendants of the ancient mystery schools—the ancient Greek and Egyptian rites as they were handed down through the ages—with doses of kabbalah and Christian mysticism thrown in. Ceremonial magic is a system, not a theology. The practitioner is calling on certain godforms, but these are not exclusively Jewish, Christian, Greek, or Egyptian. They are an amalgam. Perhaps the godforms would best be described as archetypes rather than specific deities.

Most of what is published today about ceremonial magic descends from the Golden Dawn, a magical group formed in the late 1880s. During the years when the Golden Dawn was active and flourishing, most of the Western mystical tradition was reviewed, revised, corrected, codified, explained, and updated by members of the group, then written down and passed on to their successors.

The lesser banishing ritual of the pentagram, or LBRP, is a grounding, centering, and cleansing ritual. I use it a lot when traveling. Once I am in my hotel room for the night, I do an LBRP and this psychically seals the room from outside psychic influences. By morning, when I am ready to leave, it has dissipated and the room is back to "normal."

The rose cross is another circle, but it is also useful for healing. *There is a warning:* do not use this ritual on anyone with an unstable heart or cardiovascular condition. The extra energy can cause problems. In any case, when doing this ritual, you can call down the energy, but let the person take as much or as little as they want. Do not force it on them.

No matter what one's tradition or training, these two rituals are useful tools in a person's magical repertoire.

Lasting Enchantment

······

by Nuala Drago

From ancient times to modern, every culture has recognized the magic of flowers. Volumes have been written about their lore, romance, and symbolism. They have been assigned planet correspondences, and meanings have been ascribed to their colors, species, harvesting, and aromas.

There is small wonder in this, for the beauty of flowers has the power to move hearts and communicate emotion without a spoken word. They vibrate with the energy of love. Their beauty and aroma has the ability to alter the atmosphere, uplift spirits, rouse passion, and incite lust.

Why then, are these most potent of blooms allowed to wither and die, to be discarded like so much rubbish? Don't let all that beauty and mystical enchantment go to waste. Preserve and use it! Flowers are easy to preserve no matter which method you choose. You can hang them dry, use a microwave, silica gel, or an oven, but the easiest method of all requires no effort whatsoever. When you are given a lovely bouquet of flowers, display them for a few days and then move them to a cool place out of the sunlight. Leave them in the display container and don't drain the water. Place some newspaper or wax paper underneath to catch dropping foliage, but then simply leave them alone for as long as it takes.

In a couple weeks, you should have some crisply dried blossoms that are enchanting symbols of your love and affection to another. Powerful tools, these. Get a pair of scissors and start snipping off the flowers, foliage, and greenery that you want to keep, and that looks attractive, making certain that each item you collect is completely dry.

You don't have to do another thing with them, but there really is so much more you can do. If you have seen the movie *Braveheart,* you know that William Wallace won his lady love's heart when he presented her with the dried thistle she had given him when they were children. Imagine, then, pressing a thin satin ribbon and a dried rosebud into the sealing wax of a love note, to be hand delivered, as a simple love charm.

Don't stop there. Why not make a batch of potpourri or sachet? If you don't wish to wait until you have been given enough flowers by your love interest, it wouldn't be cheating to add some flowers of your choice from your own magical flower garden, or add pine cones, wild ferns, herbs such as cinnamon sticks, and even the blossoms of certain weeds. Choose different varieties for the colors, their meanings to you, their foliage, beauty, size, magical assignations—whatever. Combine them in way that are meaningful to you, or use them in more traditional ways.

You can scent the mixture with your favorite oil if you wish. Be sure to use a fixative such as orris root power so the fragrance will last. You can display it in a pretty container, or tie or sew the mixture into a handkerchief, piece of lace, or satin. Tie a ribbon around it and hang it in your closet or place it in a drawer. Wear some in a locket as a love charm or fill two poppets with the mixture, one to represent you and another to represent your love. Tie them together with a beautiful ribbon and put them in a secret place.

Other suggestions for your dried flowers include such things as dream pillows, shadowboxes, circlets to wear during your rituals. These last are easily made by gluing your dried flowers and some greenery or moss to any length of satin ribbon. Adorn a hair comb, barrette, or headband. Decorate a picture frame with moss, rosebuds, and baby's breath. Some of the blossoms may be protected with a clear acrylic spray to make them less fragile.

Make floral water to use as a body splash by adding about a quarter cup of unflavored vodka to a pint of distilled water. Add flower petals and buds and a few drops of a specific oil such as rose, orange, or lavender, and keep them tightly bottled to uncover whenever you wish to enjoy their mood-altering fragrance.

Decorate candles to float in your bath water. Decorate food by using fresh, fried, or sugared flowers. However, not all flowers are edible, so consult a good book and stay with the ones you know are safe—such as organic violets, rose petals, and nasturtiums.

Imagine. Fantasize. Mental images are very powerful. Use fresh flowers as well as dried ones. I can't think of a better reason for starting your own magic flower garden. If some flowers are too exotic to grow, and it is unlikely that you will find them fresh or ever receive them as a gift from your life, don't despair. You can still buy their essential oils. Essential oils and dried flowers make wonderful incense.

There is no limit to the seductiveness of flowers if you unlock your creativity and open yourself to their magic. They are magnets for elementals and spirits of nature and will bring beauty, joy, and lasting enchantment into your life if you share their uplifting energy with those you love.

Sphinx Work

······

by Cerridwen Iris Shea

Mention "sphinx" and the image that comes to mind is the Great Sphinx near Giza, but sphinxes differ in type and in country or origin. The Great Sphinx near Giza, for example, is an *andro-sphinx*, who has a human head on a lion's body. There are also sphinxes with a lion's body and a ram's head (*crisosphinx*) and a lion's body with a hawk's head (*hierocosphinx*).

The word sphinx itself is thought to have derived from the Greek *sphingo* ("to strangle") or *sphingein* ("to bind tight"), which is the way the Greek creatures of this description dispatched their victims. The Great Sphinx of Egypt predates the Greek stories of these creatures, and it is not known what the race of creatures was originally called by the Egyptians. It is known, however, that around 1500 BCE, one of its several names was *Ho-em-akht* ("Horus on the Horizon").

One of the uses for sphinx statues was as temple guardians. Some pharaohs had their likenesses cut into androsphinx statues. Hatshepsut, one of the female pharaohs of Egypt, had many sphinx statues carved in her likeness. Most of them had their faces hacked off in the years after her death, when attempts were made to wipe her existence as pharaoh from the historical record. Some of the remains of her sphinxes can be found at the Metropolitan Museum of Art in New York City.

To stand in the room with these beautiful stone sculptures and stare at what is left of the faces is to feel the power when myth meets humanity. Power, knowledge, and sadness roll off the pieces in waves. The Riddle of the Sphinx that Oedipus so famously answered is miniscule compared to the power and knowledge stored by this stunning race of creatures.

Working with the Sphinx

Several questions have to be answered in order to work with the race of the Sphinx. The first is why do you want to work with them? What do you think you can gain from sphinx work? Power? Knowledge? Strength? And what will you do with what you receive from them? If your answer to these questions is something as simple and thoughtless as "I thought it would be cool to see what it felt like to work with a sphinx," or "I want the power of the Pharaohs" you will be greeted only with silence.

In other words, don't waste their time. Ask yourself the important questions about your life's path, your life's work, and your life's desire before you start your magical workings. You can't approach the Sphinx with any sort of wavering. The Sphinx does not guide or encourage but works in absolutes. Before going to the Sphinx with desires, you have to know exactly what they are and why you want them.

Sphinx work is about soul-purpose rather than the daily details of life. Once you've chosen a path and presented it to the Sphinx, the Sphinx won't tell you if it's the right or wrong path. It's the path you've chosen. It will tell you how you now have to earn it. You may be given riddles. You may be sent on a quest. You may be refused. Refusal doesn't mean returning to ask for the same thing over and over again. A human is not going to wear down a Sphinx. It means going back and re-examining your goals, your desires, and your reasons for them. It means dissecting the innermost parts of yourself, facing parts you may not want to see, and using them to create a whole spirit.

When working with the Sphinx, you have to earn respect on Sphinx terms, not human terms. Yelling, screaming, and waving swords or muttering spells will not impress a Sphinx. The Sphinx demands more. It demands to know your soul. You must approach the Sphinx with an open heart, a solid understanding of what you seek and why you seek it, and honesty. Don't try to hide or pretend that what you seek is for the good of all if it's merely for the good of you. The Sphinx can always smell a lie.

Once you have truly determined your desires and fully acknowledged your intentions, the question is how do you work with the Sphinx. *Answer:* Slowly, carefully, and mindfully. It's not work for someone just starting on a spiritual path. Working with Sphinx energy is something a soul needs to grow into. It comes out of emotional maturity, a sense of being grounded and centered, a wholeness, a sense of accomplishment in life, and a happiness in the things of the world. The Sphinx will not offer options when you're at a crossroads in your life. The Sphinx will wait and let you make the decision and then force you to earn passage down that path.

That doesn't mean that you can't honor and enjoy the Sphinx before you do the actual work. Keep a statue or photo of a Sphinx where you can see it often, or keep it within your sacred space. Read as much history, archaeological description, and mythology about the Sphinx as you can. Visit museums, read books, and watch documentaries. Listen to all points of view. See what resonates with you and what doesn't. If you get a chance to visit the Great Sphinx or any other such statue, do so. Feel the calm, contained, knowing energy of the centuries emanating from the statues.

While feeding your interest in the Sphinx, work on your own life. Deal with the past, create a beautiful present, and visualize a positive future. Take active steps to become the most positive, whole spirit that you can be. Take responsibility for your thoughts and actions. Treat others well. Protect, serve, and stand up for what you believe. Stop berating yourself for not being perfect; enjoy being human. Walk lightly on the planet and make a positive difference.

BUTTER LAMPS:
THE SAFE ALTERNATIVE
FOR YOUR ALTAR

......

BY DR. JONN MUMFORD

An MSNBC story on candles detailed the environmental and
personal pollution provided by some brands sold to the con-
sumer. As the follow excerpt by Francesca Lyman, from January 2001 details:

> *No one ever mentioned the controversies over burning
> candles that have flickered in the news throughout last
> year: that candles with lead wicks can give off toxic
> emissions. One study, by researchers at the University of
> Michigan, found that such candles give off emissions that
> exceed Environmental Protection Agency–standards for*

outdoor air... Don't burn candles with a shiny metal core
in the wick unless you know it's lead-free.

Given the custom of using candles for both ritual and for ambience, I would like to introduce you to the use of magical ghee, or clarified butter, in lamps as a natural source of light for your altar and other magical purposes.

Indian ghee lamps, often popularly called "butter lamps," provide a very pure, very nontoxic flame that make splendid focal points in magical ritual. Ghee lamps are perfect for use as altar lamps and are wonderful for romantic interludes as well. The flame is nontoxic and pure, and gives no smoke when properly adjusted. It also is part of an ancient magical tradition.

Ghee, or clarified butter, is a delicious, if cholesterol-laden, substance preferred for Indian cooking. Ghee is a semiliquid form of butter from which the water and milk solids have been removed by heating and straining. Indians refer to it as "liquid gold," and it can be bought at any Indian market in larger cities. (The recipe for turning unsalted butter into ghee also appears at the end of this article.)

The Lamp

Providing you live in a city with an Indian ethnic community, it would be simplest for you to go to an Indian shop to purchase your ghee lamp, and the cotton wicks appropriate for the size and type of the lamp. There are two types of ghee lamps; one variety is a shallow *yoni* dish, in which ghee and a special cotton wick is placed and lit. These lamps may be made of brass or clay. The other type of lamp has a special wick holder in the center so that the straight cotton wick points upright, rather like a candle.

In this type of lamp you can also burn grapeseed or sunflower oils, both of which are, in homeopathic magic, sacred to Surya or the sun. Think of sun-ripened grapes and sunflowers to see the reasoning.

Homemade Wicks and Butter Lamps

Since you may not always be able to find a ready-made ghee lamp, you may have to master the fine art of making a cotton ball wick on your own. Here are the accoutrements necessary for a homemade ghee lamp: a supply of ghee, a shallow metal dish (half an inch maximum depth, no more), and pure cotton balls.

Note: I rushed out today just in case I was so out of touch with the real world that real cotton balls no longer existed. I had visions of finding only synthetic, teased plastic balls rather like cotton candy, but I discovered you can still buy real cotton balls these days. Just make sure the package says they are pure, 100 percent cotton and nothing else.

Procedure

Melt a little ghee gently in a saucepan. Remove it from the heat and drop in a few cotton balls so that they become thoroughly saturated. Remove the cotton balls and gently squeeze the excess ghee out of them. Take care not to distort their round shape, then twist the top-third of the cotton ball into a point, leaving the other two-thirds as a ball shape. The point, which will be your wick, should be no more than an inch in length.

Now, pour the remaining melted ghee into the metal container and place the ball flush up against an edge with the wick extending horizontally over the side or lip. Brass ashtrays are ideal since they have ready-made lips to hold cigarettes. Otherwise, with pliers you can make a lip in your small metal container. Remember the dish must not be more than half or three-quarters of an inch deep or the cotton ball may drown in the ghee.

Light the point, or wick, of your cotton ball, and a lovely flame will appear. When you get the knack of this, the lamp will burn on the altar for an hour or more—depending on how much capacity your container has to hold ghee.

Making Your Own Ghee

First you will need:

1 lb. unsalted butter

Break the butter into smaller pieces and melt it over medium heat in a stainless-steel or glass saucepan. Stir to encourage slow and even melting of the butter without risk of burning. While stirring, turn the heat up and allow the melted butter to reach a gentle boil. Once it is boiling, turn the heat to low and simmer. Bubbles will rise to the surface of the butter, and a foam will gather as a crust on the top. You may skim this off or leave it alone; these are milk solids, which will eventually settle to the bottom.

Allow the butter to simmer until all the bubbles stop rising (which indicates the water has been boiled off), and you are left with milk solids on the bottom and hot, clear golden oil on top. Turn off the heat source and remove the ghee with a soup scoop or ladle, being careful not to disturb the milk-sediment on the bottom. Golden ghee is the pure oil fat left over after the water has been boiled out of the butter and the milk solids have been decanted.

Assuming you have a steady hand and the pan has a handle, you may gently pour the clear ghee directly into a heatproof glass or steel container with a lid for future use. Allow to cool before sealing.

Ghee is a remarkable in that it does not become rancid and will indeed keep months unrefrigerated. Kept in the fridge, you can be sure it will last six months or longer. One very famous cook recommends freezing ghee to prolong its life to a year or more. Ghee is highly valued in Ayurvedic medicine as a restorative and a vehicle for carrying medications.

Ghee takes temperatures of up to 375 degrees F before burning, and when used for frying it gives a rich flavor. Ghee is particularly good for cooking spices, as it encourages the release of the medicinal and culinary components of them.

CHAOS FOR CREATIVITY: SPELLS TO UNBLOCK YOUR INSPIRATION

······

BY ELIZABETH BARRETTE

The tide rises, the tide falls. The moon waxes and wanes. Summer gives way to autumn's drifting leaves and winter's desolation. All things in nature have their cycles, their peaks and ebbs of energy. The same holds true for personal energy and inspiration.

It doesn't matter whether you are a writer, an artist, a musician, a handicrafter, or a hobbyist: all creative people have something in common. They have an inner muse who inspires them to create beautiful or terrifying things, who whispers ideas to them, who fills them with creative energy—and who sometimes goes on vacation at inopportune times. Here are some practical and magical techniques for coping with creative blocks.

Causes of Creative Blocks

It can feel like a wall, something you pound your head against but can't break through. It can feel like a vast, enveloping fog that makes it impossible to find your way. It can feel like you've gone to the well only to find it dry. Whatever the subjective experience, creative blocks tend to stem from a few basic causes.

1. You're not ready to create. This is one of the most common problems, and happily the easiest to fix. Maybe you don't have an idea yet. Maybe you have an idea, but no groundwork. Inadequate preparation can stall any project. *All you need to do is finish your research:* read the source books, find the right pattern, study that new artistic style, lay out your materials. If you just need a place to start, try writing down your resource list first.

2. You're afraid to create. Fear can take the wind right out of your sails, whether you're afraid of success or of failure. Another frequent obstacle is the fear of messing up an important project. Energy work can often help you get past your fear.

3. You're trying to create entirely inside your head. Your head is where you incubate ideas. It takes your hands to manifest them. It's easy to get stuck trying to move from one to the other, so aim for forward momentum; even a little progress will help get the project into the material world where you can refine it as needed.

4. You feel too crowded to create. It's hard to produce a masterpiece with the phone ringing, the kids

crying, and supper boiling over on the stove. You need time and space free of interruptions. Consider working outside your home at a park or library or coffeehouse—or you might get up or stay up an hour earlier or later than everyone else. Magically, work on your shields to protect you from unwanted outside pressure.

5. You started in the wrong place or from the wrong angle. Back up and start over. You may be able to reuse what you've already done, or you may have to discard it and begin from scratch. Regardless, you won't make useful progress down a wrong path. A fresh start should revive your enthusiasm.

How Magic Can Help

Although practical concerns can contribute to the problem, creative block is fundamentally a metaphysical affliction. It is easier to affect mundane things through material means, and ephemeral things through mystical means. Because it works on the same place of reality, magic readily influences creativity and offers many possibilities for handling creative blocks.

First, consider your personal energy. You should be free of negative impulses from the outside, and you should have enough energy to work comfortably. Experiment to see if your inspiration flows better when you are more or less grounded, with your magical shields up or down—but you should always center yourself before you begin.

Next, consider your workspace. A warded room is best, to keep out unwanted energetic interruptions. Purify the space periodically with a sprinkle of salted water or with sage smoke. To attract positive energy, hang wind chimes, spinners, or crystal prisms in the window; keep a potted plant or small aquarium on your desk. This is also an ideal place for your muse shrine (see below).

When you work, pay careful attention to the magical implications. For writers and painters, sometimes a blank page or canvas can act as a subtle energy barrier. *You can break this "surface tension" much the same way you'd cut a door in a circle:* by touching it with the tip of your athame. Those of you working in malleable media such as yarn, fabric, or clay may find it useful to play with the material before beginning serious work. Composers and musicians benefit from communing with their instruments at the beginning of a session, warming up with their favorite tunes according to mood, and so forth.

Finally, spellcraft provides a more methodical means of restoring and maintaining your inspiration. The following spells deal with different aspects of creativity. Each relates to one of the five causes of creative block, as described at the beginning of this article.

Divination for Creativity

To avoid running out of ideas and to always have a place to turn for fresh inspiration when you want to begin a new project, you can make a simple divinatory set to give you a random selection of concepts. Writers, teachers, and other people whose creative outlet involves language may want a collection of words, such as a jar of tiles from a magnetic poetry set. Painters, graphic designers, and other visual artists may prefer a set of pictures, such as loose magazine clippings. Knitters, scrapbookers, and other handicrafters should have luck with a box of miscellaneous supplies (balls of yarn, paper squares, etc.) that can suggest a color or style. Musicians and miscellaneous creative folks can find any of the above options useful.

For this spell, you will need your creative divination tool, an incense burner and lighter, and a stick of incense. Inspiring scents include neroli, sandalwood, clove, ginger, or any blend named something like "creativity." Light the incense and waft your divination set through the smoke three times. Each time say, "I charge this tool as a container for my creativity." Then hold the tool and concentrate on its energy and potential. Let the incense burn out on its own.

Whenever you need ideas, draw three objects from the set and combine their concepts in a project. You might wind up writing a poem about flowers, bridges, and juggling; or sculpting a candleholder featuring dogs and children. You can do this ritual twice, and then combine two or more divinatory sets—for instance, words and colors. Draw one or two items from each set. In this case, you could compose a tune inspired by lightning and the color violet.

Confronting Your Fear
Doubt, hesitation, worry, trepidation, stage fright, timidity, panic—by any other name, fear remains one of our most formidable obstacles. We can feel it, yet we can't touch it. Part of its formidability comes from its very formlessness. So one of the best ways to disempower fear is to give it a material form.

For this spell, you'll be making a physical manifestation of your fears. (This is best done away from your home or other primary workspace.) Use any symbol of something that holds you back. If you're a writer, you might make a papier-mâché figure out of rejection slips. If you're a sculptor, you might build a sand-castle to represent your self-doubts. A good option for anyone is to write or draw your worries on a scroll, roll it up, and tie it with a black ribbon for binding. As you create this object, concentrate on pouring all your fears into it.

Sit for a while with your symbol, and acknowledge the effect that fear has had on your life in general and your creativity in particular. Then destroy the object. You could burn it and scatter the ashes, if it's made of paper. The tide will naturally come in and dissolve a sandcastle built on a beach, and so forth. Imagine your fears magically disintegrating along with the object. Feel them lose their power over you, leaving you free to create. Watch until the symbol is completely destroyed, tidy up the area and dispose of any garbage in an appropriate receptacle, then walk away without looking back.

Honoring Your Muse

Inside every creative person lives a divine spark of inspiration. This muse gives us ideas and guides us as we bring things from the realm of mind into the realm of matter. This same energy can help when you get stuck at that juncture. It helps to have a special place for invoking your muse.

Start by creating a shrine for your muse. A small table, shelf, or corner of a counter is ideal. Cover it with an altar cloth of gold (for revelation), blue (for communication), red (for creative power), silver (for dreams and inspiration), black (for receptiv-ity), or other colors with special meaning for you. *Add symbols of your creative success:* copies of your work, letters of acceptance, contracts, sales slips, thank you notes from satisfied customers, compliments from people who have admired your material, pictures of yourself creating, etc. You could even include an image of the nine muses from ancient Greece. Leave room at the front and center of your space.

For the spell itself, you'll need nine white candles (tea lights work well) and holders, a lighter, and a vase full of colorful flowers. Begin by putting the flower in the vase as an offering. Light the first candle and say, "I give thanks to my muse for bringing creativity into my life." Light the second candle and make a request or wish, such as, "I ask for the energy to complete my new project by this Friday." Light the third candle and give thanks again. Continue alternating thanks with requests. Light the ninth candle and close with thanks, saying, "I give thanks for all that I have created in the past, and all that I will create in the future."

Spend a few minutes meditating on your own muse. Allow the candles to burn out on their own, if practical, or extinguish them when you're done meditating.

You Can Do It in Your Sleep

Creativity springs from the subconscious, and one of the best ways to access it is through dreaming. Your sleeping mind roams free of constraints that could block your creativity in waking space. I've been using my dreams for inspiration for many years, and more than once I've awakened with an entire poem or story in my head ready to be written down.

For this spell, decorate your altar (or your muse shrine) in deep, dreamy colors such as blue or violet or silver. If you can find a star-spangled altar cloth, so much the better. You will also need a moon-shaped candle; if you can't find one, a regular candle in a moon-themed candleholder will also work. The most important part of this spell is the item you use for your dream focus. A dreamcatcher is one good choice. Find a blue or violet one with turquoise, amethyst, or jade beads; a quartz point is another ideal decoration. (You can dab a dreamcatcher with a drop of jasmine or peppermint oil for visionary dreams.) Alternately, you could use a dream pillow; these are often made from celestial-themed fabrics, stuffed with rice or buckwheat hulls and herbs such as bay (inspiration and wise dreams), mugwort (visions), mullein (repels nightmares), rose (happy or clairvoyant dreams), and white sage (attunement to the spirit world).

Work this spell after dark, shortly before you go to bed when the moon is waxing. Light the moon candle and say, "My inspiration waxes like the moon. As the moonlight fills the night, so creativity fills my dreams." Take hold of your dream focus. Feel its shape, smell its scent. Let your subconscious mind learn to recognize it. Imagine this object guiding you to new and exciting ideas. Fill it with your power. Say to your dream focus, "I give thanks to my muse for my creativity. With this dream focus, I summon refreshing sleep full of splendid visions and inspiration." Meditate on this idea for a few minutes, and then extinguish the candle. Hang a dreamcatcher over your bed or take a dream pillow to bed with you when you go to sleep.

Three Impossible Things before Breakfast

Sometimes you just get stuck in a rut. When that happens, you need to get unstuck—you need something to jolt yourself out of the rut. In Zen meditation, the master may whack the student with a bamboo stick to startle him out of his ordinary thought patterns. But you don't need to get hit with a bamboo stick; you just need to do something slightly outrageous.

For this spell, you will need three beads, large enough (three millimeters or half an inch, or bigger) to handle easily. Choose either clear quartz, which can be "programmed" for any magical purpose, or glass in whimsical shapes that you find inspiring. You will also need a tassel and some colored cord or ribbon—wild neon, rainbow, gold, or silver are good choices. String the beads one at a time onto your cord, knotting it between each bead. Then tie the cord closed with the tassel hanging at the end. You may size it as you wish: keychain, bracelet, and necklace sizes are all effective.

This spell works best when performed in the morning before you eat; food is a grounding influence, so avoiding it for a little while helps access your intuitive mind. But if, like me, you're really not a morning person, you can do the spell later in the day.

Put the beads in your pocket and go out. Do three outlandish (but not dangerous) things. Make them things you would ordinarily never do. Visit an art museum or listen to music of a style you usually avoid. Pretend you don't speak English (or whatever the local language is) and try to order coffee. Wear all your clothes inside out or backwards. Go into an ethnic restaurant or pastry shop and eat things you don't recognize. Use your imagination! (If your imagination refuses to wake up and play, try asking for suggestions from the first five-year-old you see.) For each outrageous thing you do, touch one of the beads. Infuse the bead with the energy of that moment when you experience something totally unexpected, that sudden jolt of sensation when you leave behind what you knew for what is new. Remember to eat breakfast after you finish charging the beads, if you didn't work it into the charging process.

Next, take your fully energized beads to your creative work-place. Lay out your supplies. Think about how "stuck" your in-spiration has been, like a car in a rut. You know how you get a car unstuck, by rocking it back and forth? Rub your fingers over the beads like that—forward one bead, back of one bead, forward two, back two, forward all three—gathering the energy as you go.

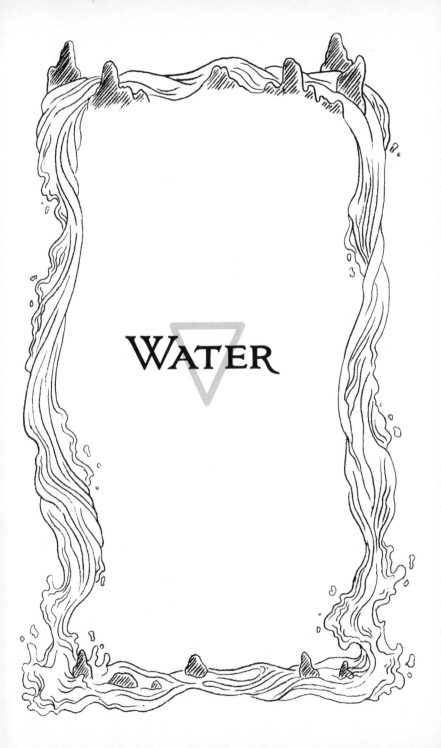

WATER

SUPERSTITIONS
CONCERNING THE MOON

······

by Raymond Buckland

If the first time you see the new moon it is straight ahead of you or to your right, it is said that you will be very lucky for the next month. If it is to your left, it will be an unlucky month. If it should be behind you, it will be the worst possible luck.

If you should first see the new moon through a windowpane, it is unlucky. In some parts of England it is said that the bad luck will take the form of breaking glass, since you saw the moon through glass. Gypsies consider it unlucky to see the new moon through the boughs of a tree, but in this case, the bad luck can be broken by immediately taking a coin from your pocket, spitting on each side of it, and holding it up to the light of the moon.

An old English superstition had it that the first person in a group who saw the new moon should kiss one of the opposite sex and say what he/she most desired. The object would shortly be received, it was said. Another superstition has it that if you are alone you should kiss the first person that you meet, of the opposite sex, to obtain what you desire.

An eleventh-century English manuscript says that if you approach the king when the moon is only one day old, the monarch will grant whatever you request. Later books modify this to say that whatever you wish for, on first seeing the new moon, you will receive before the end of the month (or the end of the year, in some areas). Gifts are frequently associated with the new moon in many countries.

In Scotland men and women would bow and curtsy to the new moon when first seeing it. In other parts of Britain people would kiss their hand to it. In Ireland the people would kneel and say, "May you leave us well and safe as you found us."

The new moon was frequently taken as a good time to do divination, especially for finding out who you would marry. A seventeenth-century manuscript says: "The first time you see (the new moon), hold your hands across, saying this three times, 'New moon, new moon, I pray thee tell me this night who my true love will be.' Then go to bed without speaking any more that night and you will certainly dream of the person you are to marry." Another contemporary manuscript says you should say, "All hail to thee, moon, all hail to thee! I prithee, good moon, declare to me, this night, who my husband must be." Two examples from the nineteenth century are from Scotland and from Berkshire, England: Chambers's *Popular Rhymes of Scotland* states, "The young women of the Lowlands, on first observing the new moon, exclaim as follows, 'New moon, true moon. Tell unto me if [insert name], my true love, he will marry me. If he marry me in haste, let me see his bonny face. If he marry me betide, let me see his bonny side. If he never marries me, turn his back and go away.'" While in Berkshire the maidens go into the fields, look up at the moon, and say, "New moon, new moon, I hail thee! By all the virtue in thy body, grant this night that I may see he who my true love is to be." They will then see their "true love" in their dreams that night.

Another form of divining one's "true love" is to hold up a black silk handkerchief between you and the moon while you pray to see your lover. Also, by looking through such a cloth, it often appears that you are "seeing" more than one moon. The number you see is an indication of the number of months or years that will pass before you marry. One ancient book instructs that the querent go to a stream and "hold a silk square over the water with the moon behind you. The silk diffuses the light and several little moon reflections appear in the water. The number of moons denotes the number of months you must wait before becoming a bride."

Perhaps most superstitions connected with the new moon are to do with money. As far back as 1507 AD, in *Gospelles of Dystaues*, we are told, "He that hath no money in his purse ought to abstain him from looking on the new moon, or else he shall have but little all along that moon." Many books, before and since that time, have instructed to be without money at the time of the new moon is to be in for a very hard time, if you look at the new moon. Some writings are specific about the money being silver. In other words, if you have no silver in your pocket, you will be unfortunate no matter how much copper or gold you have.

Turning the money you have—especially silver—is very important at this time. On the first day of the new moon when you first see the moon, you must put your hand in your pocket and with eyes closed, turn over the coins. Some say specifically that you must turn only the silver; some say it should be the smallest coin in your pocket. In Devonshire, England, you are expected to shake your pocket to turn the money in it. In some areas you are instructed to actually take out the money and hold it up (and turn it) in the light of the moon. The turning of your money is to encourage it to increase during the coming month. In the north of England they really take no chances—there you are expected to take out your money, turn it over, turn yourself around three times, and make a wish!

Full Moon

Although most Neopagans and Neowiccans associate the moon with the goddess, in fact in many countries (e.g., Germany), the moon is regarded as masculine, from which we probably get the idea of "the man in the moon." *The Harley Manuscript of 1340 AD* refers to him: "man in the moone stand and strit; On his bot-forke his burthen he bereth." Similarly, Shakespeare (in *A Midsummer Night's Dream*) has Flute speak: "The Lanthorne is the Moon; I, the man in the moon." In *Household Tales*, a popular book at the turn of the century, we find: "The 'man in the moon' is said to have a bundle of sticks on his back, and it is said that he was put there because he gathered sticks on a Sunday."

Regardless of the sex of the moon, it has always been considered unlucky to point at it. In Lancashire, England, it is recorded as "a sin to point at the moon." While the above-mentioned

Household Tales states, "If you point nine times at the moon you will not go to heaven."

Much magic is done at the full moon or when the moon is increasing (waxing) to the full. A manuscript of the mid-1600s states: "The most easy delivery a woman can have is always in the increase, toward, and in the full of the moon, and the hardest labors in the new and silent moon." Aubrey, in 1688, said: "According to the Rules of Astrology, it is not good to undertake any business of importance in an eclipse (of the moon)."

In Somerset, the belief is that a child born in the waning moon will need far more care and attention to survive than will a child born in the waxing moon. Shaw's *History of Moray* (1775 AD) states that "the druids avoided, if possible, to fight till after the full moon."

In Scotland it is unlucky to marry during the waning cycle of the moon. It is also unlucky to move house unless: "…the moon be waxing, the tide be flowing, and the wind blow on the back of the person who removes."

Trees cut down during the full moon produce harder wood than those cut in the waning cycle, according to Welsh beliefs. Also, fruit and vegetables gathered at that time will last longer than those gathered in the waning cycle. A similar belief holds throughout much of Europe regarding the planting of crops; they need to be planted in the waxing cycle, unless they are root crops, in which case they may be planted when the moon wanes.

It can be dangerous to sleep in the light of the full moon, according to many old beliefs. A seventeenth-century work warns: "When thou goest to bed, draw close the curtains to shut out the moonlight." Another book, written 200 years later, states, "Human beings are said to be injured by sleeping in the moon's rays," while a twentieth-century work mentions, "As children we were cautioned against going to sleep with the moonlight shining on our faces. We were told that if we did, we should go blind."

However, moonlight can be very beneficial as, for instance, the removing of warts. There are several traditional wart-removing cures that involve holding the hand or other afflicted part in the light of the moon. A seventeenth-century book states: "For warts we rub our hands before the moon." Another contemporary work says, "One should offer to wash his hands in a well-polished silver basin wherein there is not a drop of water, yet this may be done by the reflection of moonbeams only."

Similarly, it is traditional to "charge" a crystal ball or other scrying tool by exposing it to the light of the full moon.

Seashell Spells
for Your Health

......

by Janina Reneée

When concentrating on mental imagery for bodily healing, it is helpful to use visual and tactile objects that inspire the unconscious mind. Seashells can be used as symbolic objects to assist some visualizations. Certain shells have been likened to body parts, and their pleasing shapes and glossy surfaces also suggest lustrous health and beauty.

For dental care, smooth, glossy white shells suggest perfect teeth. For example, if cavities or sensitive teeth are a problem, place such a shell before you as you treat your teeth with a fluoride gel or rinse, or even while sipping milk or green tea. Visualize the fluoride or calcium doing its work to help repair the enamel shell of your teeth. Visualize your enamel becoming thicker, stronger, and healthier.

If you have a shell that has both white and pink surfaces, use it to visualize healthy teeth and gums. As you brush, mentally recite the words "bright white teeth, perfect pink gums," glancing at the shell to reinforce your imagery.

For improved hearing, gather shells that are associated with hearing. Ears are sometimes described as shell-like; the cochlea, the part of the inner ear that is responsible for hearing, resembles a small shell. Some Moon snails and abalones are referred to as "ear shells." And, of course, we fancy that holding a shell to the ear allows us to hear the call of the ocean (though this is actually ambient noise trapped and bounced around inside the shell). For any sort of hearing problem, you should always seek proper medical care. However, for some minor problems, such as impaired hearing due to allergies or colds, low-level ear infections, mild intermittent cases of tinnitus or Meniere's disease, cysts and other obstructions in the ear, and normal diminution of hearing due to the aging process, you can complement your treatment with the following exercise.

Hold a shell up to your afflicted ear or ears, listening as best you can to the oceanlike roaring within. (Medium-sized conch shells may get the best results.) *Visualize yourself by the side of the ocean, your attention fully attuned to the sound of rolling waves, and then recite to yourself:* "In this vibration, the song of the ocean, a song of healing, restore my hearing." Imagine the sound waves transformed into waves of psychic energy, vibrating your inner ear in a way that restores its optimum functioning, setting everything right. If the exercise causes the slightest pain, desist at once and seek medical treatment. (Persons with mild cases of Meniere's and other balance problems should perform it sitting down.)

For reproductive well-being, cowries have been valued as amulets for good health throughout the world. Aside from their beauty, cowries bear resemblance to several body parts. Because their long ventricle slits suggest half-closed eyes, cowries are used as facial features in African and Middle Eastern masks and figurines. Their apertures also resemble mouths or vulvas, and the general shape of a cowrie is similar to a uterus. Thus, the Romans called them "little wombs," and in Japan, the cowrie is known as the "easy delivery shell." Women giving birth hold one in each hand to ensure a successful and healthy birth. Associations with fertility are also seen in their group name *Cypraediae* (in honor of Aphrodite, called the Cyprean because legend said she was born on the island of Cyprus). Cowries found in prehistoric graves may have been symbols of rebirth.

If you are a mother-to-be, try stroking a cowrie while saying affirmations such as "Smooth and easy; easy delivery." The white eggshell cowrie is ideal for this purpose. To promote general feminine health and pride in sexuality, any woman could caress a cowrie while beaming some loving energy to her reproductive organs.

In regard to bone health, the calcareous composition of the corals, as well as the stems and branches of certain species, calls to mind a skeletal structure. In fact, some calcium supplements are derived from coral. If you are concerned about osteoporosis or healing a broken bone, you might enjoy contemplating a piece of coral while taking your daily calcium supplement and mentally reciting "Strong body, strong bones. Strong body, strong bones." In addition to stimulating the unconscious mind, handling a seashell engages the conscious mind, handling a seashell engages the etheric "virtues" of the minerals in the shell.

For mental power, consider brain coral. While investigating the magic of the Deep South during the Depression, Zora Neale Hurston studied under a man known as Father Watson, who was renowned for removing curses. Watson's wife believed that the source of his power was a large piece of brain coral that he kept on his altar. Brain coral (species of the genus *Meandrina*) have folds and ridges that resemble the convolution of the human brain. A piece of brain coral can inspire students, creative people, and others whose work require mental activity.

To amplify your brainpower, spend a few moment contemplating a piece of coral. Allow your gaze to follow its valleys and ridges. Trace them with your fingers. Relax your eyes as you take in its larger patterns. Feel that you are becoming calmer and calmer, yet also more alert, as you explore its convolutions. If there is a special question on your mind—perhaps you need the solution to some problem—state it aloud, and then continue to contemplate the coral. After a few moments, set it aside. If the answer has not already popped into your mind, have faith that unconscious forces have gone to work on it. For persons who suffer from certain minor forms of nervous or neurological problems such as sensory processing disorder that affect learning abilities, regular contemplation of brain coral might help modulate mental energies.

If you enjoy the beauty of seashells, you will no doubt think of many additional ways to use them for healing magic.

Some Divine Figures of the Seas

......

by Marian LoreSinger

Isis

Isis is associated with water because she is portrayed as traveling in a stone-carved moon boat in her temples. Her name may have originated from *Ashesh*, which meant pouring out or life giver. She is a womb or mother figure. One of Isis's tears was said to have flooded the Nile.

Poseidon

The Greek version of Neptune, pictured holding a trident, Poseidon was not one of the gods acclaimed for his virtues. He (or his priests) was lustful of earthly kingdoms. In myth he often took territories from various forms of the goddess, including an attempt to take Athens from Athena.

Poseidon's origins were less than potent. Early lore called him the spouse of the earth. He only became a god after these early associations were forgotten. Most of the stories of Poseidon center around him trying to outsmart or overcome the goddess, and thus reflect an age-old struggle between the sexes.

One story of Poseidon recounts a time when he tried to flood the Xanthin plain. The women there decided to oppose Poseidon by marching upon him with their genitals exposed. Poseidon, in a sudden burst of wisdom, chose a hasty retreat!

Mari

Known as Marian, Miriam, Myrrhine, etc., this particular goddess seems to have counterparts in every portion of the world. In Egypt, Mer was the goddess of water and a symbol of maternal love. In northern Europe, Maerin was the wife of Thor. Please note the similarity to the name Merlin, a mage whose life was closely linked with the grail, a potent water symbol. In Saxon mythology, Maerin was known as Wudu-Maer.

Mari dominated what is now known as the Holy Land until 1700 BCE. Here, her name was often combined with the male aspect of the sun to become Meri-Ra in Egypt or Mari-Yamm to the Hindus. She was pictured as a great fish that birthed the gods. This image was later translated into the mermaid. Mari is also one of the earliest versions of the trinity in that she was not only mother of the sea, but also the earth and heavens. As the goddess of the grove, she was Maid Marian to the Celts, beloved of Robin, and archetypes of the Horned God of witches.

In Sumero-Babylonian traditions, Mari closely corresponds to Tiamat, the goddess mother whose name means deep or womb. Even in Israel, Mari was once worshiped in her own right as the consort to Yahweh.

Magical Correspondences? What Do I Use Them For?

......

by Silver RavenWolf

Almost every how-to magical book on the market gives you listings called magical correspondences. These lovely tables and columns brim with neat and nifty information that may include the subjects of herbs, planetary influences, candle colors, angels, gods and goddesses, metals, moon phases, magical alphabets, incenses, stones, etc. You'll find daily correspondences, weekly correspondences, and monthly correspondences. With all this information, every single spell of magical application should work perfectly, right? Wrong.

The word correspondence (in magical applications) means stuff that goes together, things that match, symbols whose energies blend well with each other, or ideas that carry historical representations. These symbols enhance the practitioner's planned application. For example, the color red vibrates close to the same energy frequency as the emotion of passion. Historically, the color red conjures an association with the element of fire, and is associated with the root chakra. The heart shape travels through the collective unconsciousness as a symbol for love. Mythos, created by the human mind, tells us that Aphrodite stands for that elusive energy known as love. The soft scent and vibrational pattern of a rose blends easily with thoughts of love. Make that rose red, cut out a red paper heart to depict the fires of passion, call on Aphrodite, and you have the makings of a simple spell for conjuring love with the help of the correspondences you chose: red, fire, heart shape, and Aphrodite. Through these symbols the magical practitioner uses sight, smell, touch, and emotion to focus on a chosen desire—love. If we throw in a full moon or a waxing moon, we've added a planetary body whose energies affect the chemistry in our human bodies, and again, the full or waxing moon finds historical association—lovers trysting under a full moon, and the waxing moon's association with growth.

Correspondences don't make the magic—you do. Consider the correspondences as fine-tuning devices, or that special ingredient in your favorite dish that gives the food an extra zing. Although correspondences carry energies of their own, their function relies on your focus. Throwing a bunch of stuff together (as in our previous example), a red candle, a red paper heart, rose petals, calling on Aphrodite on Friday in the hour of Venus during a waxing moon, won't secure the love you need by itself. Correspondences help you to focus on your desire initially. Correspondences have energies that you can manipulate. The more correspondences you use in your magic, the better chance for success if you remain focused on the application, and if the universe has determined that your goal should manifest. Since not all goals and desires would be good for you, the universe may not dispense the energy in the way you wish, or in the time frame you desire, no matter how many correspondences you use.

Must you use correspondences in your magical and ritual applications? No. Some factors do override the energies of a correspondence. Emotion, for example, plays a big part in magical workings. If your need carries a high emotional level, such as how you feel during an emergency, and waiting for the right correspondence (the moon phase or the correct planetary hour) isn't possible, your energy level may override the need for the use of those types of magical correspondences.

Magical training will also enhance the use of correspondences. If you have learned to focus, practice routine meditation exercises, work with energy flow in the body and in other areas, have a good relationship with spirit, etc., then these aspects of your training will enhance the use of correspondences.

Magical correspondences work well in our times of fallow, when our energy level feels low. Every individual experiences slow periods, and sometimes these vacant stretches can last six months or more, depending on the various issues and entanglements in our lives. In these times, the more correspondences you use, the better your chances of success in a magical or ritual application.

Must you use only the correspondences listed in magical books? Nope, although I'd work with these correspondences first to get the hang of what I'm doing. After you find your comfort zone with already published material, learn to create your own correspondences, but do so carefully. Experience on a small scale and work up to bigger projects. Any spell book you buy represents someone's (usually the author's) experimentation with various correspondences.

Some correspondences will work better for you than others. Magical practitioners have found this particularly evident in color magic. Certain colors vibrate better or can be massaged easier by one person than another. Again, this circumstance depends on magical training, experience, social background, personal history, and individual energy flow—all the factors that make you an individual.

Don't let those lists and columns of magical correspondences confuse you anymore. Take your time, experiment, and build your skill level with the tried-and-true methods, as well as your own. You won't regret it!

CREATING A MAGICAL FORMULA

······

by RAVEN GRIMASSI

Everyone wants to perform spells and works of magic with consistent and reliable results. There are essentially five so-called "ingredients" that comprise the art of creating successful works of magic. You can adapt them or arrange them according to your own needs as long as you employ them all. These components are personal will, timing, imagery, direction, and balance. Let's look at each one and gain an understanding of the concept.

Personal Will

Personal will can also be thought of as motivation, temptation, or persuasion. In order to establish enough power to accomplish your goal, you must be sufficiently moved to perform a work of magic. If you do not focus fully on the results, or if you invest only a small amount of energy in your desire, you are unlikely to realize any true results. The stronger your need or desire is, the more likely it is that you will raise the amount of energy required to manifest what you seek. However, desire or need is not enough by itself. Bear in mind the desire must be controlled, and the will must be focused only upon a detached view of the desired outcome of your spell or magical rite. Enflame your mind in the intent while at the same time separating yourself from the desired result. In other words, run the race mindful of the finish line but totally focused on the pace.

Timing

In the performance of ritual magic, timing can mean success or failure. The best time to cast a spell or create a work of magic is when the target is most receptive. Receptivity is usually assured when the target is passive. People sleep, corporations close overnight and during holidays, etc. One must also take into account the phase of the moon and the season of the year. Wiccans always work with nature and not against her. Generally speaking, four a.m. in the target zone is the most effective time to cast a spell of influence over a person or a situation.

Imagery

The success of any work also depends on images created by the mind. This is where the imagination enters into the formula. Anything that serves to intensify the emotions will contribute to the success of your spell. Any drawing, statue, photo, scent, article of clothing, sound, or situation that helps to merge you with your desire will greatly add to your success. Imagery is a constant reminder of what you wish to attract or accomplish. It acts as a homing device in its role as representation of the object, person, or situation for while the spell is intended. Imagery can be shaped and directed all according to the will of the Wiccan without detracting from focusing the mind on the spell's intent. This becomes the pattern or formula that leads to realization of desire. Surround yourself with images of your desire and you will resonate the vibrations that will attract the thing you desire.

Direction

Once enough energy has been raised, you must direct it toward your desire. Do not be anxious concerning the results, because anxiety will act to draw the energy back to you before it can take effect. Perform your spellcasting with the expectation that the magic will work, accept that it has, and simply await its manifestation. Reflecting back on the spell tends to ground the energy because it draws the images and concepts back to you. Once the spell is cast, mentally detach yourself and try to give the matter no more thought so as to not deplete its effectiveness. Mark a seven-day period off on your calendar and evaluate the situation seven days later. It usually takes about seven days (one lunar quarter) for magic to manifest.

Balance

The last aspect of magic one has to take into account is personal balance. This means that one must consider the need for the work of magic and the consequences on both the spell caster and the target. If anger motivates your magical work, then wait a few hours or sleep on it overnight. While anger can be a useful propellant for a spell, it can also cloud the thinking. If possible, make sure you have exhausted the normal means of dealing with something before you move to a magical solution. Make sure you are feeling well enough to work magic and plan to rest afterward. Magic requires a portion of your vital essence drawn from your aura. Replenish this with rest even if you do not feel tired. Health problems begin in the aura long before the body is aware of them.

Henna Magic

······

by Sybil Fogg

Henna smells like dirt and is cold when applied to skin. The eucalyptus oil used to prepare the skin smells like life and is pleasantly warm. When combined with incantations, a full moon, and expectant parents, henna can create some potent magic.

Early in my fourth pregnancy, the life of my unborn child became threatened. My midwives were at odds: one thought that my pregnancy would not declare itself and another felt that bed rest and reduced stress could allow the pregnancy to continue.

When those measures didn't work, I decided to use henna magic. I felt handing over the fate of my unborn child to the goddess and god was a necessary step to remove stress from myself. I had already followed all of the recommendations of my midwives to no avail. I needed something that would help me focus my energy away from what was happening to me and direct it toward making something happen for me. That is what magic is all about.

It also helped that my partner is a skilled henna artist.

Henna art is called mehndi and draws its traditions from the Middle East and India. The action consists of applying a thin coat of a paste made from ground henna plant mixed with black tea and eucalyptus oil. There are many variations in the recipe with people trying a little of this and a little of that to find the desired consistency. Personally, I find that mixing equal amounts of henna powder and brewed black tea with a quarter amount of eucalyptus oil creates the best paste. For example, mix a half tablespoon of eucalyptus oil with two tablespoons each of henna power and black tea. Henna paste should have the consistency of toothpaste.

Henna works by staining the skin. This happens almost immediately, but to assure a darker, longer-lasting design, it is best to coat the henna with sugared lemon water and to leave it on for at least eight hours. Once dry, henna can be brushed off. A cotton ball dipped in olive oil can be used to loosen any stubborn residue. The image that is left will be light to dark reddish-brown depending on the color of your skin.

Henna magic is powerful. You are using earth to draw your intention from your own body. It incorporates all aspects of spellcasting, from mixing the powder to creating the design to applying the paste to your skin. Henna magic should be approached with extreme care and respect, for you will be wearing your design for about one month, the time it takes the moon to go from round to dark to round again. As with anything being applied to your skin, you should test a small area first to be certain that you won't have any reactions to the henna paste.

To begin any magic, you should first determine the nature of your intention. In the case of my possible miscarriage, mine was specific. I didn't want to lose my baby. Henna magic can be used for any type of spell: prosperity, love, self-confidence, happiness.

Once the nature of your spell has been decided, it is important to choose the correct correspondences to go with your magic. The day, time of month, and astrological influence should be researched and observed. In my case, I chose to do my spell during a full moon to represent the pregnant goddess and picked a day that the moon was in its governing sign, Cancer, because I wanted all influences to be as strong as possible for my request.

When choosing your time, keep in mind that mixing henna paste is time consuming. You will need about two days to make the henna, one twenty-four-hour cycle to brew the black tea (two tablespoons in one cup of hot water) and then another twenty-four-hour cycle once the paste is mixed. Once ready, the prepared henna will only last three to four days, so timing is critical.

It is useful to add a pinch of certain herbs to your henna mixture. Be sure to check your lore and to grind the herb into powder so that it is absorbed into the mixture and doesn't clog up your applicator (the easiest vessels for applying henna are plastic tubes used for silk screening found in most art supply stores). A coffee grinder works well to grind the henna with the herbs, but make sure you clean the grinder thoroughly or purchase one solely for spellcasting. There are many books on herbal use in magic if you are having trouble choosing. To keep the henna paste smooth, use a minute amount of only one or two herbs. For example, I used lavender for protection of children and rose petals for love in my spell.

Once you have determined all correspondences direct your intention to the design. Are you simply going to write out the words of your spell? Perhaps this is not what you want to wear for the next four to six weeks. Maybe you will settle on symbols to represent words. Or one image. For my spell, I let my partner create a more traditional Indian motif in which he inscribed symbols representing our intentions.

Once you have your henna paste and your design picked out, you will need to choose what part of your body to decorate. If you are working solo, you are pretty much limited to your feet, legs, or the hand/arm opposite your writing hand. If you are fortunate enough to be working with an artist, then the options are limited only by your body and the nature of your spell. Because of the circumstances, I chose my navel.

Now that you have everything you need and all is planned out, it's time to do some magic. Start by casting a circle in the way you normally would. Feel free to call the quarters, though this is by no means necessary. When I do magic, I like to burn incense and candles appropriately scented and decorated to my intent. Then I call the quarters and cast my circle, at which point I drawn down the moon by reciting my version of "The Charge of the Goddess." It is in the center that I chant for what I want while my partner applies the henna. When finished, we both say, "From full to dark to full again, please grant for us (me) our (my) wish by then" over and over raising the cone of power, inhaling deeply with the words. Once we are filled to the brim, we release the cone by exhaling loudly. At this point, blow out the candles, close the circle, and thank the guardians of the four corners. The henna will last for the moon's cycle if care is taken not to scrub vigorously while washing, wearing gloves for dishes (if the design is on the hands), and keeping the area dry. As the henna dries, your wish will come to fruition. In my case, I am now the proud mother of a son born at the Winter Solstice of 2005.

ACTIVATING YOUR
PSYCHIC AWARENESS

······

by Karen Follett

Psychic ability has a long history. Much of this history is engulfed in mysticism and secrecy. Palmists, mediums, crystal gazer, and those who read divinatory tools have been involved in this history since its origins. Still, while psychic ability is a part of society, it is often viewed, unfortunately, as separate from the mainstream, and this dictates a "those who can" versus "those who cannot" mentality, regarding accessing the knowledge that exists beyond our tangible world.

The Truth About Psychic Ability

While the concept of the "extraordinary" and "unique" ability regarding the psychic realm is a fabulous marketing strategy, it is inaccurate to think that only a "special few" people have the ability to perceive psychic information. The ability to see, hear, feel, and know the psychic realm is extraordinary, unique, and special.

But this ability is no more extraordinary that the ability of every living creature on this planet to perceive the world around us.

Psychic ability, which is also known as precognition, clairvoyance, and intuition, was given to our ancient ancestors by the divine creator. The ancient's wisdom regarding the perception of the oneness that exists between themselves, their universe, and the divine opened their psychic awareness. The ancient's day-to-day incorporation of spiritual beliefs into mundane existence furthered their psychic skills and perceptions.

Since that time, eons of "evolution" have brought us into the "civilized" world of today. Our encapsulated existence in cities, suburbs, and housing tracts has caused us to separate ourselves from nature. The grind of work, social and personal responsibilities, and daily modern living all too often tend to leave us with little time to attune to the universe and its creators. As a result of this "evolution," we have become more accustomed to using our analytical skills and less accustomed to tuning in to our psychic skills.

Regardless of this conditioning, psychic ability remains a part of our genetic code. While some people seem to be more naturally plugged into the psychic circuit, it is important to know that the wiring is present in all of us. It just may need reconnecting.

Rewriting Yourself
for the Psychic Realm

The fact that you possess a (perhaps latent) psychic ability is the first step in developing your psychic potential. The next stop is to ask the universe to help you reconnect your psychic circuits.

Since we exist in a tangible, visual world, it is helpful to state to the universe an action that will initiate your "psychic circuitry." This action could be the visualization of flipping on a switch or turning a dial. Or it could be an actual physical act such as anointing or touching your third eye.

The creation of such a switch connects the physical world and our basic selves to the spiritual world and our higher selves. The "switch" also helps in turning off or toning down the psychic circuit when you are in situations of psychic overload. Two tools that are essential to aid in your reconnection to the universal "oneness" of our ancestors are guided imagery and meditation.

Guided imagery is communicating to the universe. By imagining a mind's eye scene with focused intent, you communicate your desire to the universe. Utilize guided imagery to state your intent and create the environment that will be conducive to the second tool of meditation.

While guided imagery is communicating to the universe; meditation is listening to the universe. Relax your body and open your quiet mind. "Listen" to the universe and the message that are being sent. Open the "message centers" of seeing, hearing, feeling, and knowing.

Psychic communication can come in a variety of forms. You may see images of symbols. You may hear words or sounds; you may feel emotional or physical sensations. Or you may have a "gut" feeling that just informs you of something.

Particularly in the early stage of reconnection, some of this communication may seem confusing or insignificant. Don't worry about interpretations at this point, just accept the perceptions as they are given. As mentioned before, the guided imagery and meditation act to reunite you to the universal oneness.

Once you feel comfortable with your reestablished relationship with the universe, you will be able to ask for and receive symbolic interpretations of this information. You will also notice that you can set your psychic circuit to the "comfortably on" mode, and receive perceptions without constant use of formal guided imagery and meditation.

Psychic Journaling

Please note that I intentionally used the words of "constant" and "formal" in the previous statement. Regardless of how tuned in you become to your psychic ability, there will be times when guided imagery and meditation are priceless.

The next step in the psychic reconnection process is to begin a "psychic development journal." Your initial use of the journal will be to document any perceptions that you received during the meditation session. To begin your journal, keep your "psychic circuit" connected and record what you visualized, heard, felt, and suddenly knew. Again, don't analyze, but ask the universe if there are any interpretations that it would like to send to you at that time.

After you have completed your journal entry, thank the universe for your reconnection and close your psychic circuit. As tedious as it may sound, writing in your journal will prove to be an invaluable tool, regardless of how adept you become in your psychic development. The act of writing tends to occupy the analytical brain and leave the perceptive brain open to receiving messages.

In the end, your journal will provide tangible proof of your progress in psychic development. You will also be able to refine your perceptive abilities by documenting perceptions and outcomes.

Reality, both tangible and psychic, is a matter of personal perception. The psychic messages sent from the universe are pure. We are human. As humans we have the innate ability to take a pure perception and alter the interpretation to meet our own perceptions of reality (or desired reality). By documenting perceptions and sensations noticed with your senses, you will be able to discern a true psychic interpretation.

Keep in mind that psychic hits and misses are just a part of life. I once read that even the psychic cream of the crop experiences only about 80 percent accuracy. More often than not, this 80 percent reflects the most important element of the universal reconnection process. Meaning, that since psychic perceptions reflect a static situation in a universe that is ever flowing and changing, there is no absolute accuracy in perception. Any action or inaction can set the flow to alter outcome.

Psychic ability is an ever-changing gift from an ever-changing universe. The assimilation of this concept is the last step in psychic development. Reconnecting your "oneness" to the universe and the acceptance of their psychic gifts will ensure that you will flow as she flows, you will grow as she grows, and you will respect her laws of karma and balance in the use of her gifts.

THE PAGAN PAST OF
IRELAND'S OLDEST SYMBOL

......

BY EDAIN McCOY

The wee little shamrock, the tiny trefoil clover of vivid green, which grows in abundance on the Emerald Isle, has a long and cherished Pagan history, as well as a legacy of magical uses.

Modern Irish lore tells us it was St. Patrick who brought the shamrock to notice by likening it to the holy Christian trinity of father, son, and holy ghost. Long before he catapulted the shamrock into prominence as Ireland's principle emblem, it was honored as the symbol of the power triple goddess: maiden, mother, and crone—three separate deities yet one. In Irish mythology, the shamrock is linked to three important goddesses: Airmid, a goddess of herbal healing; Eire, the goddess for whom Ireland is named; and Dechtere, who alternately takes on the images of maiden, mother, and crone throughout her myths.

As a magical herb, the shamrock (*seamrog* in Gaelic) has been used for a host of beneficial purposes. To add a touch of Irish luck to your magic, try any of these ideas:

- Use the little trefoil as a focus to help you align with or invoke the triple goddess.

- The shamrock can be used as a catalyst for magical healing by helping you draw on the powers of the goddess of medicine, Airmid.

- Fresh shamrocks are irresistible to friendly faeries. Irish lore tells us they also make great bait for capturing Leprechauns.

- The white variety of shamrock makes a superb protective talisman when carried or sewn up into protective charms.

- Shamrocks can be set in windows to psychically purify the room and protect the window.

- The verdant green of shamrocks makes them a natural in money/prosperity or fertility spells. You can efficaciously replace any other herbs in these spells with shamrocks.

- Carry shamrocks in your pocket when going on a job interview to give you a leg up in the job-hunting process. (But beware! They may also bestow upon you the gift of Blarney.)

- The shamrock is the original of the belief about four-leaf clovers being lucky. If you find a four-leaved shamrock—a rare mutation—you should make a wish. Then bury the sprig, sealing the spell in the earth by making three clockwise circles above it.

- Most of all, shamrocks are very, very lucky. Ever heard of the "luck o' the Irish?"

Snow Magic

......

by Silver RavenWolf

So there you sit. The snow falls in rich flakes, then turns into a blinding fury. Is there magic in snow? You bet there is!

The snowflake epitomizes the crystalline magical womb of the All Mother—Holda or Hela. She represents the unity of all patterns. Within the structure of the snowflake all things form and evolve. Mother Holda has the mysterious powers of death and life. Her wild and destructive energies undulate in chaotic patterns, yet command deep respect.

Snowflakes crystallize in the shape of the ancient "hex star" symbol, which stands for cosmic wholeness and complete structure. This symbol, called the "hexefus," means witches' cauldron or witches' foot (the root of the witches' power). Therefore, snow magic can be a blessing or a bane, depending on how you use it.

Dame Holda commands and uses the "roads between the worlds." She flies among the "ghost roads" at night with the Gandreid, her ghostly company of witches and spirits. The goose flies beside her, an emblem of this spirit-flight. Snowflakes fall from the bird's wing feathers upon the world below, as the goose passes overhead at midnight. Mother Holda directly represents crone magic and the wisdom of grandmothers. Therefore, snow magic falls under the auspices of the dark mother. Here are some simple magics to try with snow:

- To melt hard feelings against you, gather snow that has fallen in a gentle storm. Write the name of the person who is giving you a hard time on a piece of paper. Put it in the middle of a glass plate. Take the snow and pile it on top. Add a dash of sugar. As the snow melts, the person in question will loosen his or her hold over you.

- To banish someone or something that has given you a lot of pain, take snow from a wild storm and follow the same procedure as in number one. Be sure to ask for Dame Holda's blessing and that the spell not reverse or place upon you any curse.

- Snow poppets are fun to make. If a friend is sick, fashion a tiny snow person, add something that belongs to him or her, such as a lock of hair. As the snow melts, your friend will get better.

- Instead of using your athame, cast a circle with one of those splendid icicles.

- Make snow wishes. With your staff or wand, carve your wishes in the snow. Ask Dame Holda to grant your wishes. Trace the hex star beside the wishes to seal them.

- Make a snow bottle. Write your wishes on a piece of paper and put the paper in a bottle packed with snow. As the snow melts, your wishes will be granted.

Magical Ethics for Teens and Their Parents

......

by Estelle Daniels

Magic and Wicca are everywhere these days—on TV, in the movies, and in books of fiction and nonfiction. It's so popular that many people have become very interested in learning more about, and possibly becoming part of, the tradition. Unfortunately, though, having an interest and willingness to learn does not guarantee you will be able to find a good and ethical teacher.

Tips for Beginning Your Studies

The first thing you should know about magic is that what is depicted in popular media is not at all like the real thing. In the years I have been a practitioner, for instance, I have never met anyone who could merely wave their hand and cause things to happen. The truth is magic is much more subtle and slow-acting than would ever serve a Hollywood plot. In the movies, the actors only have a short time to get done what they want to get done, so of course magic is made to appear more dramatic, visual, and quick than it is in real life.

In truth, magic and Wicca are studies that can be pursued and perfected over a lifetime or more. As with most worthwhile things in this life, no one book or secret recipe will be able to make you an instant expert. Becoming a magic-worker takes practice and intensive labor. Of course, there are many aspects of magic that you can master in a short stretch of time—such as learning to read tarot cards, for example, or learning a simple incantation. But these are just small facets of the magical life.

Creating a Magical Life

Many people who choose to become magical find they create a magical life for themselves. They begin to view the world differently, paying attention to things others might miss. Their ideas, values, and priorities change and become somewhat different from more mainstream people.

Of course, a magical person still has to go to school or work in order to bring food to the table, but these workaday trappings of modern life can take a back seat to knowledge and experience in the magical realm.

That said, the most effective way to learn about things magical and Wicca is to find a solid, ethical teacher or become part of a good and nurturing group. Of course, this sounds easier than it is. Few groups advertise for members, and the best groups are relatively small and have little turnover. Classes are available here and there, but not all are accessible in terms of time or sometimes money. Plus, the exchange of money does not necessarily bring ethics into the matter—in fact, often the opposite is true.

Teaching Magic to Teens

A further complication occurs for teenagers who, inspired by what they see on TV perhaps, want to learn about magic and Wicca. Many teachers won't teach minors; this is not out of prejudice, but rather for solid legal reasons. In the past few years, parents, grandparents, and stepparents have all sued and won cases against people teaching their children about Wicca and magic. The law in our society makes children the sole responsibility of their parents, and if the parents don't want a child doing something, any adult who helps work against that can be sued or criminally prosecuted. Alternatively, some teachers may have parents or guardians sign a waiver before they take minors on as students. This is for everyone's protection in the event of a future litigation.

If you are under eighteen and want to learn about magical traditions and the religion of Wicca, your options are somewhat limited as far as finding a teacher. Still, there are many things you can do on your own. First, look to attend any public lectures, seminars, classes, or book signings that you can. If there are psychic fairs in your area, go and watch, ask questions, and observe. Some people are willing to talk in informal settings, even if they refuse to take you on as a student. Any event open to the public is a safe work zone for the exchange of information—in other words, parents will have a hard time suing a teacher for the information they give in a public lecture.

Of course, at these events, you might have to pay an admission price. Do so, and feel free once you are there to talk to people. Be friendly and eager to learn. Don't be a pest. Respect boundaries but ask questions. Sometimes you can get into conversations and learn things. You may even ask an elder if they might meet you and talk to you over lunch—again, in a public place. Always be sure you can pay your own way.

If people are busy or can't talk, don't take it personally. Just move on and keep trying. Occasionally you will find someone who is willing to talk and teach you informally. There is certainly no harm in trying.

If you find a metaphysical bookstore in your area, go there and ask the employees if they know of any classes or open groups. Ask them for help and advice. Sometimes they will be more than willing to share. Furthermore, you can just go and browse the books and listen to the conversations of customers. You might be able to pick up some interesting information; at the very least, you will get some useful reading done. If you can, try to get a part-time job at the store. Working in a place with such materials on hand, and with such customers, is a great way to pick up a magical or Wiccan education.

Certainly, as you already must know, you can learn much about magic and Wicca by reading books. But these sources are not intended to be the end of your education. You should also go beyond the books by trying to practice things yourself. Don't be afraid to experiment. If you cannot find a teacher, get a few friends together and work it out among yourselves. Don't be worried about looking or sounding strange. Simply keep your activities private. Don't impose your beliefs or practices upon those who aren't interested or might be uncomfortable. Wicca and magic are part of your private life, and though they may seem wonderful to you not everybody will feel the same. Cultivate discretion; it will serve you well in the future.

Read magical fiction too. This is not to say that if you read all the Harry Potter books, you can become Harry Potter. We all would love that, but it isn't possible. You may think fiction is simply at best an interesting and diverting pastime, but you should know too that reading such material does train your mind to think in magical ways. Reading about magic and spells can get your mind used to understanding what it might feel like to do magic and Wicca.

Be careful to choose positive and helpful literature, not the darkly horrific or negative stuff. In your books, look for people who are active, who take care of themselves, and who make a positive mark on their world. If you like Harry Potter, there are many other books in the same vein. Ask your librarian or bookstore clerk. They will probably have a list of other books and authors to read. The genre is called science fantasy, though it covers much more than just magic. Realize that when you read, as when you watch TV or movies, these are fantasy worlds, and things are exaggerated for plot and effect.

Okay, you can also continue to watch your magical movies and TV shows too. Again be careful to choose the positive ones, and be sure not to become dazzled by the special effects and quick plot resolutions. As mentioned before, real-life magic does not reach its fruition so quickly and neatly. Life is a lot less flashy and takes a lot longer to resolve. Sometimes things don't even get resolved or even solved—that's life.

Finally, in your studies you will find there is a lot of information on the Internet. Be careful here. The most effective people generally don't have time to hang around chat rooms, and frequently the people who are the loudest and boast the most know the least. Information on the Internet isn't always reliable.

Unfortunately there are few restrictions here. If you find a cool website with loads of "secret" information that nobody else has, be cautious. If their stuff is so secret, why are they putting it on a website? If someone says on their website that they know best, and everyone else is wrong, be wary. Do your research; take your time; do not commit to anything—especially if a website asks for money before they dole out the truth. Usually the only truth you learn is that a fool and their money are soon parted. The Internet is anonymous, and many shady people rely on this anonymity to do their shady deals. If it feels wrong or bad, just say no and go elsewhere.

Your Own Ethics

As you begin to learn more, here is a word of advice: be careful about proclaiming yourself to be an expert simply because you have read a book and practiced a bit. There are people who have devoted many years to study and practice, and nothing turns others off faster than the instant expert.

That is, try to keep an open mind about other people and their opinions and practices as you learn more about what you like and what works for you. Just because you read a book that makes one claim, don't assume all other approaches are wrong. Different people have different ideas. Be open to know different ways of doing and thinking about things. Listen and think about what someone says before automatically saying they are wrong. At the very least, express your thoughts in the form of an opinion: "I think you might be mistaken," or "I got different information from this book."

Magic and Wicca should make you feel good about what you do and make your life better. Be patient, and learn what you can. Many of us started the same way, and we are still around. Good luck.

Parents and Wicca

If you are the parent of a teen who has expressed an interest in magic or Wicca, there are many things you can and should do to help your teen. Your key role might well be to check things out to be certain your child is getting good, reliable, and honest information.

My first and best advice to parents is this: do not panic. After all, the majority of teens who are interested in these subjects eventually go on to other pursuits. It's a fad. If you don't make a big deal of it, they will either stay with it out of honest interest, or find something else to freak you out.

Next, you might be well served if you do some research. If your teen is reading books about magic and Wicca, read some yourself. How do they seem to you? You will likely be surprised how harmless they are, and how positive and motivating. If they scare you because they clash with the beliefs you were brought up with, take a look at the underlying mindsets. These practices, like most religions or spiritual pursuits, are designed to make a person more self-aware, motivated, thoughtful, helpful, caring, sensitive to others, and interested in making the world a better place. As a result, the practices of magic and Wicca may suddenly seem not as awful to you. You might realize you are simply objecting to the way things are done, rather than the mindsets.

Still, there are bad people everywhere, and Wicca and magic are no exceptions. Focus your attention on the individuals your child is associating with—as opposed to the mindset of the spiritual practice. Be certain to watch for attitudes or practices that are selfish, dominating, nihilistic, destructive, or encouraging of practices that are dangerous to self and others. Separate the individuals from the general practice, and be sure to talk to your child about these things.

If your teen is on the Internet, be sure to monitor their activities. Ask about the websites they have visited, and look at them yourself. Lurk in a few chat rooms and monitor what goes on. Most of the time it's just boasting and bravado. Be sure to let your child know that you will continue to take an interest and that you will not tolerate any bad practices or behavior.

If your child sends away for materials or goes to classes, look at the materials yourself. If your teen wants to take a class with a private teacher, check the teacher out. Call and ask about what will be taught and what goes on in the class. Ask to sit in. Some teachers won't teach minors at all. Some teachers require parents to sign a waiver granting permission for a minor to study. If the teacher won't talk with you or if you get a bad feeling, err on the side of caution. It will be difficult to give your reasons to a teenager, but if you are uncertain about the particular practices of a teacher or group, you will have to tell your child to wait until they reach adulthood and can make the decision alone. The anger and frustrations your child may feel after this is preferable to having him or her get into a bad group and be damaged.

If there is a great deal of money involved, be extremely wary. Most Wiccans for religious reasons cannot charge for teaching the craft—outside of reimbursement for supplies and books. Few people will teach magic for a fee, and if one promises to teach everything quickly, you have special reason to be skeptical. It just doesn't work that way.

If your teen finds a teacher that you agree may be good, you should ask many questions: what will they be teaching; what books will they use; how long the course will take; what the work-load and time commitment will be for your teen; what the rules are, and what your child will have to commit to; what you as a parent will have to commit to; how long the teacher has been teaching; how many students are in the class; and where the class will meet (though rules about secrecy may prevent the teacher from saying exactly). You may even want to ask for references.

You might not get full or understandable answers to these questions, but use your instincts. The teacher may speak in jargon, but listen to their tone and attitude. Are they upset that you are checking up on them? Are they resentful, secretive, misleading, or obfuscating? Those are not good signs. Are they patient and willing to answer your questions? Do they seem knowledgeable, have credentials, and are willing to let you sit in? Those are good signs.

Wicca is a religion, and becoming Wiccan means choosing a religious path. This is of course not something to be taken lightly. If you don't want your teen changing religions, discuss it. Give your reasons openly, and be fair to your child. Expect the same from him or her.

If you object to magic, examine your reasons. Is it because you are afraid your teen will blow your house up? Are you afraid they will be possessed by demons? You should know this is silly—these things just don't happen. The worst thing that will happen if a spell is done incorrectly is nothing. Do you object to magic in and of itself? Why? Most magic these days is done for healing or self-help. Prayer itself is a classic form of magic. The practice of Wicca and magic differs very little from the ancient practice of praying—though it is much more involved.

Ask your teen why they want to get into magic. If they want a quick fix or love spells, inform them this is not how magic works. It takes time and energy, and the practitioner also has to put their energy into making the desired outcome happen. Tell your child that you would be much more impressed if he or she focused on becoming more presentable, cultivating some manners and social graces, and being a person people would like to be around.

Both Wicca and magic require work, study, and commitment to be effective and successful. Many teens when confronted with the work involved are less than enthusiastic. It certainly isn't like it is in the movies and on TV. Harry Potter depicts the amount of work, study, and practice fairly realistically, though the subjects or effects you can achieve are rather heavily exaggerated.

If you let your teen explore and read some books—and there is a whole lot of reading involved in magic and Wicca—chances are they will learn something and will eventually move on. Neither magic nor Wicca has an instant formula for success. Tell your child to be patient and open-minded, and let them know that you intend to do so too. If anything, your tolerance will teach your teen a valuable lesson.

A Family Imbolc Ritual

......

by Twilight Bard

Picture yourself a farmer in northern Europe hundreds of years ago. In the depth of winter, the fields are frozen and your food stores are running frighteningly low. Firewood stocks are quickly depleting. You watch helplessly as your children, pale from lack of sunlight and growing thinner by the week, wake up each morning crying from limbs numbed by the chill, and go to bed at night complaining of rumbling stomachs. Each day is a struggle for your family's survival against hunger and cold.

Then something begins to change. Slowly the days grow noticeably longer. The sun, like an old friend, comes back to melt the frost that envelopes the land. The season of lambing comes abruptly, bringing a new, much-needed food source: milk. Suddenly optimistic that your family will make it through the winter, you begin preparations for the new growing season.

The story above describes the spirit behind Imbolc (literally "ewe's milk"). No longer as dependent upon the land for survival as our Pagan ancestors, we now celebrate this holiday on February 2 as a time of renewal and purification. Following is a simple ritual that even a family with young children can celebrate together.

Imbolc Ritual

Gather your family around a small, glowing lamp just after dusk, and turn off every other light in the house. If your family keeps to a more formal tradition, you can cast a circle, call quarters, and invoke gods and goddesses here, but it is not necessary. Have on hand a cup of milk (it can be animal, soy, or rice, depending upon your preference) and a broom (preferably a ritual broom decorated with red ribbons).

If your children are willing to sit and listen to a story, tell them a seasonal, age-appropriate tale. Or you can simply tell the story of the season as described above. After the story say:

We celebrate Imbolc tonight,
And welcome the feast of waxing light!

Hold up the cup of milk and say:

In the shortest days and darkest nights,
There always remains a spark of light.
Father Sky and Mother Earth,
Provide for all with life's rebirth.

Take a sip of the milk, and pass the cup around for everyone to have a taste. Say:

Now the light is lengthening days,
Let us brighten our home, and set each lamp ablaze.
To the dark and the winter we bid goodbye,
As the sun comes back to brighten our lives!

Encourage the children to turn on every light in your house. Try to have at least one light in every room. Let them get excited and race about to perform the task. When they meet back in the ritual area, cheer for the light's return. Hold up the broomstick and say:

Farewell to the winter! Farewell to the cold!
In with the new, out with the old!
Greetings to the light, bright and warm,
Goodbye to the dark! Negative energy be gone!
If hereabout any lingers or creeps,
It shall be banished as the besom doth sweep!

Allow the children to take the broom into every room of the house and "sweep" every corner and nook. Sweep the walls, the ceiling, even inside the closet. The broom doesn't actually have to touch anything, just instruct them to sweep at the invisible bad energy hovering about your home. They'll know where to find it. Let them take turns, and help the smaller ones so that in their excitement they don't knock things over or break anything. Sweep your pile of negativity toward a door leading out, flinging it open and sweeping away all the unwanted energy. Give yourselves a cheer for your accomplishment.

Afterward, come back inside and play some lively music if you like, clapping and dancing together in a circle. Or, you can tell more stories or let the children put on a little skit enacting an Imbolc myth. Hold a ritual feast with dairy foods such as yogurt or ice cream. Close the ritual in your traditional way, or just let the celebration continue for as long as everyone is enjoying it. Don't forget to shut off all the lights afterward.

TWELFTH NIGHT CAKES

······

BY LILY GARDNER

There is an old practice of not allowing wheels to spin from the Winter Solstice until Twelfth Night on January 6. This custom mirrors the halting of the sun at solstice. Life seems to hang suspended during this time, and the veil between the worlds thins.

During this period of darkness and storms, horrible monsters, called Kallikantzaroi, with goat ears, blackened faces, red eyes, and long nails, hide themselves in the dark corners of cellars and barns. They come out at night, breaking furniture and devouring food stores.

Whatever they don't eat they destroy. Werewolves, said to be the grown children who were born on the twelve days of Christmas, roam the roads and murder hapless travelers. The skies contain dangers as well. The Wild Hunt, led by Frau Holda or

Wodan, is a fierce hunting party of demons souls that rides the winds during storms from Samhain to Candlemas. Any stranger wandering the roads can be swept up and forced to ride until the end of time.

Kallikantzaroi, werewolves, and the Wild Hunt are all personifications of the old year, and as custom dictates, we have to banish the old year now. When the old year is disposed of, traditionalists perform ceremonies to ensure good luck for the new year, with the principle that "well begun is well ended."

One practice to ensure good luck is to make a Twelfth Night cake. Twelfth Night ends the Christmas festivities for many people. For the most luck, everyone in the household, from eldest to youngest, must stir the cake with a wooden spoon in a deosil, or sunwise, motion. Wood is the symbol of manifestation. Each person closes his or her eyes and makes a wish for the New Year while stirring.

It is traditional to sprinkle the batter with charms for sympathetic magic, in the belief that like attracts like. Through the years, this practice of putting charms in the cake became a method of divination.

The British spring a coin, a thimble, a button, and a ring into their Christmas pudding. The thimble and button foretell that you will lead a solitary life; a ring predicts marriage, and a coin means wealth.

The French drop a bean, a pea, and a baby figurine into their Twelfth Night cake batter. The recipient of the bean is crowned king of the party; the pea-finder is crowned queen, and the lucky person who finds the baby is guaranteed a year of good fortune (and has to bake the Twelfth Night cake next year).

Some suggestions for the modern Pagan to add to their Twelfth Night cake include an almond for happiness, a cinnamon stick for abundance, a coffee bean for astuteness, a tiny fan for change, a whole nutmeg seed for love and fidelity, rice for fertility, ginger root for zeal, a key for opportunity, and a paper clip for partnership. Use charms that are safe in the oven's heat, of course, and make sure you urge your guests to play with their food so as not to bite or swallow their fortunes.

It is also possible to insert the charms after the cake is caked if you wish to frost your Twelfth Night cake (see recipe below). *Note:* The almond paste in a Twelfth Night cake needs to cure for one week before the cake is made, so please take that into account when you're planning your Twelfth Night festivities.

Twelfth Night Cake

This European cake recipe is more like our sweet bread than what is thought of as cake in the United States.

1 package yeast

⅛ c. lukewarm water

1 c. milk, scalded and cooled to room temperature

1 tsp. salt

½ c. melted butter

1 egg yolk, beaten

3 c. flour

¾ c. almond paste

Various Twelfth Night charms

Melted butter

Powdered sugar

Dissolve the yeast in the water. Mix in the milk, salt, melted butter, and beaten egg yolk. Add flour, and mix so that the dough forms a ball. Let it rise for forty-five minutes. Work in the almond paste with your hands, and shape the cake dough into a ball. The paste will be stiff, so mix as thoroughly as you can. Stuff the charms into the dough at this time. Place the ball of dough onto a parchment-lined cookie sheet, cover with plastic wrap, and let rise for another thirty minutes. With a sharp knife, cut a pentacle across the top of the ball of dough, and then bake the cake for 25 minutes in a 375 degree F oven until the surface is golden brown. Let it cool off and brush the cake's top with melted butter. Sprinkle powdered sugar in the carved pentacle. (Or you can add your favorite frosting if you prefer.)

The Wheel of the Year

......

by Pauline Campanelli

The wheel of the year is a circle without beginning or ending. The wheel of the year is the magick circle of time.

In some Pagan traditions the year is considered to being at the Vernal Equinox, when the hours of daylight exactly equal those of the dark and begin to increase. In other traditions, the year begins at Samhain (Halloween) in mid-autumn, when the dark is greater than the light, becoming greater still. And in still other traditions the Year Wheel begins at the Winter Solstice (Yule), the darkest day of the year when the dying sun is reborn.

No matter when the wheel of the year is considered to begin, its turning is an expression of the eternal cycles of life, death, and rebirth, and the celebrations of its sabbats, solstices, and equinoxes are symbolic ritual expressions of the turning points in this these cycles.

In some Pagan traditions the goddess, or female principle in nature, is perceived as immortal, while the god, or male principle, dies each year and is reborn. The goddess and the god are equal and both are eternal, though in different ways. In this same tradition the symbol of eternity—the circle—is identified with the goddess, while the wheel of the year—born in winter or in spring and dying in autumn—is identified with the god. In other traditions, however, the goddess and the god each preside over half of the year, one stepping back to allow the other to step forward. Here, both the wheel of the year and the corresponding magick circle are divided into two equal halves, each half the domain of the goddess or the god. In either case, points on the wheel correspond to points on the circle.

To begin with, the Vernal Equinox and Autumnal Equinox correspond to the directions of east and west on the circle. A line drawn through the circle from east to west divides it into two halves of the north and the south. These halves correspond to the dark half of the wheel of the year (from the Autumnal to the Vernal Equinox) and the light half (from the Vernal back to the Autumnal Equinox).

The dark half of the wheel, or the winter months and the northern portion of the circle, represents the realms of spirit and the dwelling place of the dead presided over by the Horned God. The light half of the wheel, the southern portion of the circle, symbolizes the world of matter and physical life, rules by the goddess. The eastern point on the circle signifies rebirth, while the western point represents death. The northern point corresponds to Yule, the Winter Solstice, and the spiritual life, while the southern point correlates to the Summer Solstice and physical life. As the lines drawn through the circle from east to west separate the world of spirits from the world of matter, so a line drawn from the northern to southern point expresses the union of spirit and matter.

Beginning at Yule and going sunwise around the wheel of the year, the cycles of life, death, and rebirth is expressed. From Yule to the Vernal Equinox represents the first stirrings of life in the womb = spiritual life prior to rebirth. From the Vernal Equinox, or birth, to the Summer Solstice = youth. The Summer Solstice is maturity. From the Summer Solstice to the Autumnal Equinox = aging. The Autumnal Equinox is death. From the Autumnal Equinox to Yule = spiritual life.

Most Pagans celebrate all of the sabbats at night. This has been traditional (probably since the "burning times") and, in the case of the major sabbats, is correct as they are all "eves" (Imbolc or Candlemas Eve, Beltane or May Eve, Lammas Eve, and Samhain or All Hallows Eve). That is, they all represent midpoints or turning points on the wheel and thus should be celebrated at the magickal hour of midnight, as the day and the season turns. But, the solstices and equinoxes should really be celebrated at specific times of the day. The vernal equinox should be, and probably was at one time, celebrated at sunrise. The Summer Solstice should be celebrated at midday, the time when the sun is most powerful. The Autumnal Equinox really should be celebrated at sunset— the moment between the equal hours of light and dark. And Yule, the longest night of the year, should be celebrated at midnight— the moment between sunset and sunrise.

By virtue of their association with the compass points of the magickal circle, the solstices and equinoxes also correspond to the four elements. Yule corresponds to the north and therefore to the element of earth. This is completely appropriate since the element of earth is the element of both the tomb and the womb of the Earth Mother. The Vernal Equinox equates to the direction of east and the element of air, or the first breath taken at birth. The Summer Solstice is associated with the direction of the south and the element of fire—the fire of life. And the Autumnal Equinox corresponds to the western point and the element of water. Water has always been associated with the transition we call death; the process was perceived as the deceased crossing over a body of the water. Charon, the ferryman of the Greeks, carried people to the Island of the Dead; the Egyptians crossed the Nile to the Necropolis; and the Vikings had spectacular ship funerals. With all of these, water was associated with death.

As the elements are associated with the four directions and the four seasons, so are colors. The wheel of the year also can be related to the color wheel.

The color wheel does not, in fact, actually exist. Instead, the colors that we see form a band with a red at one end at violet at the other. This is only the visible range of the spectrum. The colors actually continue into the infrared and ultraviolet ranges. But the visible range of colors can be bent into a circle, and visibly this works very well.

The order of the colors on the color wheel are as follows: yellow, yellow-orange, orange, red-orange, red, red-violet, violet, blue-violet, blue, blue-green, green, yellow-green, and back to yellow.

It is traditional among colorists and color scientists to place yellow—the warmest, brightest color—at the top of the color wheel, but in order to recognize its association with the magick circle and the wheel of the year it is necessary to place it in its traditional position on the south, or at the bottom. This puts red-orange in the east and blue-green in the west with violet—traditionally the most spiritual color—in the north.

But most importantly, the wheel of the year is a series of rituals that describe the interrelationship of the god and goddess throughout the changing seasons.

At Yule (on or near December 21), the circle and the altar may be decorated with holly, fire, or other sacred evergreens. Fires are kindled to give strength to and to symbolize the returning light of the sun. This is a time for protection magick. The goddess is honored in her aspect as the divine and eternal mother, and the god is hailed as the giving child of the new solar year.

At Imbolc or Candelmas Eve (on February 1) the circle and altar may be unadorned, expressing the absence of flower or fruit at this time of year. Candles are sometimes used to light other candles as an expression of the gradually increasing light of the sun. The goddess is honored in her aspect as the corn maiden (the virgin aspect of the grain goddess) and the god is worshiped in his aspect as the spirit father. This is a time for prosperity or increase magick.

At the Vernal Equinox (on or about March 21) the altar and circle might be decorated with pussy willow, crocus, and daffodils—the first flowers. Colored eggs, symbols of the return of spring, are exchanged and ritually eaten, and seeds are blessed. This is a time for the magick of new beginnings. The goddess is honored in her aspect as Eostre, the goddess of spring, and the god is revered in his aspect as the god of fertility.

At Beltane or May Day (April 30–May 1) the circle and altar might be decorated with a great variety of flowers, although white ones are traditional, especially the blossoms of the hawthorn. A maypole, entwined by dancers with ribbons, represents the venerated phallus. This is a time for fertility magick. The goddess is honored in her aspect as queen of the May, and the god is lord of the forest. This is the celebration of the sacred marriage.

On about June 21, the altar and circle at the Summer Solstice or Midsummer might be adorned with many summer flowers, especially large yellow or gold ones expressing the strength and splendor of the sun at this time. Fires are kindled and magical herbs are gathered. Now we do magic for gaining strength, energy, and protection. The goddess and the god are honored in their aspects as the Earth Mother and sun god.

On July 31–August 1, the Lammas circle and altar may be adorned with sprays of wheat and ears of corn as well as flowers of the season. Bread is baked and ritually eaten along with other fruits of summer. This is the celebration of the first harvest—a Thanksgiving. It is a time for prosperity magic. The goddess is honored as the grain goddess, and the god is the lord of the harvest.

At the Autumnal Equinox on about September 21, the circle and the altar might be adorned with flowers and gourds and other fruits of the season. This is the second celebration of the harvest. This is a good time for magical banishing. The goddess is honored in her aspect as the all-providing Earth Mother, and the god is paid homage in his aspect as the dying grain (or sun) god.

On the last night of October, the Samhain circle can be adorned with pumpkins and gourds and the altar strewn with acorns and oak leaves. This is the celebration of the final harvest. It also is the season of darkness and of death. It is a time when the spirits of the departed, both human and animal, are invoked to join us in the circle and when communication with the spirit world, and answers about the future, are sought. Fires are kindled to give sight to the darkness. The god in his aspect as the horned one, lord of the dead; and the goddess in her aspect as the crone, teacher of the mysteries, is honored. It is the end of the wheel of the year, but every ending is a new beginning.

CAT TALES

······

BY D.J. CONWAY

Down through the centuries there have been many tales and superstitions about cats, some of them positive, but even more of them negative. The cat was considered to be an animal of the Great Goddess. When the patriarchal cultures replaced the Goddess with their god, they needed to discredit any creature that was connected with her. What happened to the cat also happened to the owl, the bat, and the raven. Unfortunately, constant propaganda turns the tide against the Goddess's creatures, especially the cat.

The following beliefs are given for the sake of interest alone. Common sense will tell any intelligent person that the negative beliefs about cats are not true. Cats are loving but independent animals who share our homes and fill our lives with joy and happiness. It is amazing that the belief that black cats bring bad luck exists primarily in the United States. In many European countries, a cat of this color is considered to bring the very best of luck into a household.

- In ancient Egypt, women wore amulets of cats so they would be fortunate in love and all things feminine. A woman who wanted children would wear an amulet of a cat and kittens. The number of kittens indicated the number of children she wished to have.

- Wives were once made to drink milk with a cat's eye stone in it to prevent them from conceiving children while their husbands were gone on a journey.

- If a black cat crosses your path and/or enters your house, it will bring good luck. This superstition may have come from ancient Egypt where the sacred cats (especially the black ones) were said to bring blessings on any house that took care of them.

- You will be extremely rich or lucky in love if you pull off a white hair from a black cat without getting scratched (Lowlands of Brittany).

- If a cat crosses your path and does you no harm, you will be very lucky. This superstition comes from medieval times, during the very era when the "devil-cat" was so hated. Because the orthodox church could not peacefully separate the people from the goddess worship and the veneration of her cats, they linked the cat with the devil. Obviously this superstition is a twisted version of the older, less negative one.

- If a black cat crosses your path, you will have good luck. The black cat is also considered to be an omen of money (England).

- If a cat comes into your house, be kind to it, and the devil will not bother you. Another medieval twist of the superstition, this also assumes that the cat and the devil are in league. By inference, if you have the devil on your side, he will go torment someone else.

- Whenever the cat of the house is black, the lasses of lovers will have no lack.

- Keep an old cat collared and chained in a shop, and prosperity will be yours. If the cat escapes, the prosperity is believed to go with it (China).

- In parts of Yorkshire the wives of fishermen keep black cats at home to ensure their husbands' safety at sea.

- In southern England if a black cat crosses the path of a bride as she leaves the church, it will be a fortunate marriage. This is still a popular English belief. Like hiring a chimney sweep to give her a good luck kiss when she exist the church, the bride may also make arrangements to have a black cat led across her path.

- An ancient Buddhist superstition states that if you have a white cat, silver will always be in the house. If you have a dark-colored cat, there will always be gold.

- A tortoiseshell cat brings good fortune (Ireland and Scotland).

- People who dislike cats will be carried to the cemetery through rain (Holland).

- If you treat a cat badly or neglect it, carry an umbrella to your wedding (Holland).

- Cats who have three colors (red, white, and black) are able to predict the approach of storms (Japan).

- To decide whether to say yes or no to a marriage proposal, take three hairs from a cat's tail. Wrap them in white paper and put this under the doorstep overnight. In the morning, carefully open the paper. If the hairs are in a Y-shape, it is yes; if in an N-shape, it is no (Ozarks).

- Cats will deliberately suffocate babies in their cribs. They will suck away the breath of any sleeping or ill person, leaving them weak or even killing them. This erroneous idea was developed during the witch frenzy and, unfortunately, is still widely held by otherwise intelligent people. Some cats will sit on your chest and get close to your face because they want attention, but they have absolutely no need or ability to suck away your breath.

- Cats carry the souls of the dead to the afterworld (Finland).

- If a cat jumps over a coffin, the soul of the deceased will not be able to find its way to heaven (Scotland).

Folklore and Legends of Wales

......

by Sharynne NicMhacha

The folklore the legends of Wales are beautiful and mysterious and offer a very rich source of information about the Celtic otherworld.

To the Celts, the otherworld was all around us. It always existed but was easier to access at certain times of year or at certain places. It was located either underground or underwater, on an island across the water, or under the sea. In Wales, the otherworld was known as *Annwn* or *Annwfn*, which may mean "inner" or "under" world, or even "not-world" (referring to the mirror-like aspects of the Celtic divine realms, which are different from our own).

Annwn could be accessed by visiting sacred bodies of water (lakes, rivers, wells) or fairy mounds (*sedd* in Welsh, *síd* in Irish). Sacred assemblies were held at these sites, and there were traditions that if one slept on a fairy mound, one would have an otherworld encounter for good or for bad (depending on one's relationship with the spirits).

The old gods and goddesses were the original inhabitants of the fairy mounds, later becoming the "fairies" of folklore tradition. However, the Celts didn't refer to them as fairies. In Wales, they were called *plant Annwn* ("the children of the other-underworld"), *gwragedd Annwn* ("the women of Annwn"), or *plant Rhys ddwfn* ("the children of Rhys the deep").

In later times, they were called *y yylwyth teg*, the "fair/beautiful family/tribe" (which may be a word play or misunderstanding of the English word fairy). They were sometimes also called *tylwyth Gwynn*, the tribe of Gwynn (a word meaning "white," "fair," or "sacred"). Gwynn ap Nudd was an early rules of Annwn, and he led the Wild Hunt for the supernatural boar known as Torc Trwyth. In one tale, he abducts a beautiful woman called Creiddylad. Arthur decides that Gwynn and another suitor must fight for her every May Day until the end of time.

The old gods and goddesses of Wales (or early Britain) were also called *plant Dôn*, the children of Dôn, who was a primal goddess or ancestress. She had a number of divine offspring, including Arianrhod ("silver wheel," a moon goddess), Gwydion (a divine magician), Amaethon ("divine ploughman"), and Gofannon ("divine smith"). Other early British gods and goddesses may have been ancient inhabitants of Annwn as well. This list includes Epona ("divine horse goddess"), Maponus ("divine son"), Belenus ("bright or healing one"), Cernunnos ("horned one"), and Taranis ("the thunderer").

One of the most famous Welsh legends about Annwn is a kind of Welsh version of the Lady of the Lake legend. Female spirits of goddesses were believed to inhabit most bodies of water (including lakes, wells, and rivers). In this tale, "Llynn y Fan Fach," a young man is tending his cattle on the banks of a lake on the Black Mountain. He sees a beautiful young woman combing her hair, appearing to sit right on the surface of the water. She is so beautiful that he doesn't know what to say or do. He offers her some of his barley bread, but she rejects it, saying: *Cras dy fara, nid hawdd fy nala*. ("Hard is thy bread, it is not easy to catch me.")

The lad goes home and tells his mother what he has seen. She makes moist bread for him, which he offers to the fairy maiden the next day. This time, though, she says: *Llaith dy fara, ti ni fynna*. ("Moist is thy bread, I do not want thee.")

He goes home, crestfallen. This time, his mother makes half-baked bread. After the lad waits all day, finally the woman appears just before sunset. She accepts the bread and agrees to this offer of marriage on one condition: If he strikes her three times without just cause, she will leave him forever. They are married and live happily for many years. The woman bears him three fine sons.

Years later, when they are going to a baby blessing, the young man taps her to hurry—this is the first causeless blow. Another time, she cries at a wedding, and he taps her again. She replies that she was crying for the young couple's upcoming troubles. Finally, he taps her when she is laughing at a funeral (the person's troubles were over), and she disappears into the lake. The husband and sons were heartbroken and wander a long time searching for her.

One day she appears to the eldest son and tells him that his path is to heal the sick. She gives him a bag full of medical cures and herbs and reveals to him the healing properties of the plants. This eldest son and his three sons become famous healers. They write down their medical knowledge (which came from Annwn) in three medieval manuscripts in the twelfth century called *Meddygon Myddfai*. This family remains powerful healers for the next five hundred years, and distant descendants of the family still uphold the tradition to this day.

As late as the 1800s, people visited the site on August 1, the day that signaled the coming of the Lady of the Lake. This date corresponds with a Celtic feast day known elsewhere has Lugnasad, the beginning of the harvest. Other wonderful folk customs took place in Wales during the year:

Candlemas: Candles were lit in the windows to symbolize the coming of spring. Sometimes two candles were lit on the table, and each member of the family would take turns sitting on a chair between the candles. After taking a drink from a drinking horn or goblet, they would throw the vessel backwards over their head. If it landed upright, it meant long life.

May Day *(Calan Haf):* People gathered on a hilltop or village green and created a small mound on which a musician sat. It was decorated with oak branches, and people danced in a circle around the mound. Fires were lit from nine types of sacred wood, and the house was decorated with hawthorn, rowan, or birch.

Midsummer: A sacred pole or tree called the "summer birch" was raised in each area and guarded all night long against theft by another village. In the morning, people danced around the birch. There were also bonfires and divination. St. John's wort and mugwort were used to purify the home.

Winter's Eve *(Calan Gaeaf):* Special bonfires were lit from fern, gorse, straw, and thornbushes. Apples and root vegetables were roasted, and then there was dancing, shouting, and leaping through the flames. Spirits like Ladi Wen ("white lady") or the Hwch Ddu ("black sow") were believed to be about on this night.

New Year's: Early on New Year's morning, a vessel of spring water was sprinkled on people's hands and faces using a sprig of holly, rosemary, myrtle, or another evergreen plant. A procession called the Mari Lwyd ("gray mare") went from house to house. A decorated horse skull on a pole led the way, and a spontaneous contest of poetic skill was held at the door of each house.

These Welsh customs are a wonderful source of tradition and inspiration to include in your celebration of the turning of the year wheel.

MAGICAL BATHS

......

by MARGUERITE ILSPETH

While working in a little botanical shop several years ago, I learned from the owner as he prepared magical baths and bottled them for his customers. Being predisposed to "Kitchen Witchcraftikin," as my husband calls it, I was making my own in no time.

Magical baths can be used alone or with a spell. When used alone, the bath become the work, while in spellwork, a ritual bath will prepare you physically and spiritually for your spell. I usually prepare my baths at night—I find it easier to focus that way, and it makes for an enjoyable evening of magic.

For the four methods I recommend, you'll need a slow cooker or large pot (preferably ceramic or glass), a large bowl (or two bowls, depending on your method), a lid, a knife, cheesecloth or a fine strainer, twine, herbs selected for your goal, and the purest water available. Cleanse your tools with sea salt before beginning your work.

Sun Method

Fill your container half full of water and add the herbs, breaking or cutting them to the appropriate size. Cover the herbs with more water and cover the container with a glass lid. Place the container in a sunny area for the better part of a day.

Stovetop Method 1

Fill your pot half full of water and add the herbs. Add more water to fill the pot, cover with a lid, and heat to near boiling. As soon as the water begins to bubble, remove the pot from the heat and let the contents steep for several hours.

Stovetop Method 2

Place your herbs into a ceramic bowl. Pour boiling water over the herbs and cover the bowl with a glass lid. Leave this to steep for several hours.

Slow Cooker Method

This is the method I use most often. Fill the ceramic insert half full of water. Add your herbs and cover with more water. Place the lid on top of the cooker and turn the heat to the lowest setting. Leave the cooker to slowly steep the herbs most of the day.

If you are working indoors, your home will fill with the aroma. This is one of my favorite parts of the process. Light candles and listen to music, read a book that corresponds with your goal, or even write out your spell on parchment. Everything you do during the creation of your bath can become part of the magic itself, if only you decide.

When the herbal water has turned a deep, dark color, like a strong tea, it is ready. The next step is to strain the herbs from the water. Stretch cheesecloth over a large bowl and secure it with twine, or use a strainer fitted across the top of the bowl. Carefully pour your infusion into the bowl through the cheesecloth or strainer.

When I use a cloth, I untie it from the bowl after straining the herbs and squeeze out every drop of liquid I can before burying the herbs in the yard. (If you do not have a yard, you can bury them in a flowerpot). Nothing negative is being created here, so burying the herbs in a flowerpot or garden will just give them magical compost. Please don't toss them into the trash. To me, that shows disrespect for the herbs and the properties you obtained from them. You can store your infusion in the refrigerator for a few days, but it will sour quickly.

Using Your Magical Bath

Prepare a sacred space in your bathroom before you take your bath. (If you do not have a bathtub, you can pour the herbal water over your head in the shower.) Be sure to have a clean and tidy environment, so scour that tub and clean the floor. A cozy robe and a fluffy towel are also recommended.

Place candles wherever you desire, and perhaps set up a small altar on a table beside the tub. Music is usually a good thing, so if you won't be able to hear your stereo while you're in the bath, consider bringing a CD player into the bathroom to help set the mood. Burn a smudge stick in the room to cleanse out all negativity, and seal the room. This might mean that you are restricted to having your ritual bath at night after everyone is asleep, but many times that is best anyway.

Take a shower or a bath to become physically clean. Drain the tub and rinse it out. Next, fill your tub with comfortably hot water and settle in. Pour the magical bath into the tub, making sure to warm it first if it has been in the refrigerator—the last thing you want is the shock of chilly liquid poured into your bath! Swoosh the water around, blending it well with the herbal infusion. Visualize your goal and see it in everything you do. Know that the properties in this bath are assisting you in your outcome.

If your goal is spiritual cleansing of negativity or physical healing, visualize the bath drawing out impurities and rendering them benign. The longer you soak, the more you remove. It is important that you submerge your head at least once. If this is not possible, use the bowl that contained the concentrated bath to pour the water over your head. Lay back, relax, and enjoy your sacred space. This is an ideal time for meditation.

When your work is finished, pull the plug and stay in the tub as the water drains. The heaviness that you feel as the water drains away is the perfect, relaxing peace that results from a successful endeavor. If it is difficult to force yourself to get out of the bathtub, then stay for a while! Enjoy your sacred space until you are ready to leave.

After your bath is complete, dry with your fluffy towel and don your cozy robe. Leave any ritual candles to burn out or remove them to another sacred space if they will take more than the evening to finish. Your skin will be scented with the herbs, and this is another way the bath reinforces any work. The scent becomes another element of your work as it helps you to retain focus.

If the bath was your work in whole, clear your sacred space and have a wonderful night's rest. Vivid dreams are common afterward, so you may want to keep a dream journal beside your bed. If you have used your bath in preparation for a larger work, you can proceed with the rejuvenation and empowerment obtained from the simple magical bath.